Collins

AQA GCSE 9-1

Combined Science Trilogy Foundation

Practice Papers

Mike Smith, Sunetra Berry, Lynn Pharaoh, Kath Skillern and Paul Lewis

Contents

SET A

Biology: Paper 1   3

Biology: Paper 2   23

Chemistry: Paper 3   43

Chemistry: Paper 4   63

Physics: Paper 5   79

Physics: Paper 6   99

SET B

Biology: Paper 1   123

Biology: Paper 2   143

Chemistry: Paper 3   163

Chemistry: Paper 4   183

Physics: Paper 5   207

Physics: Paper 6   227

ANSWERS   247

Acknowledgements

The author and publisher are grateful to the copyright holders for permission to use quoted materials and images.

All images are © HarperCollins*Publishers* and Shutterstock.com

Every effort has been made to trace copyright holders and obtain their permission for the use of copyright material. The author and publisher will gladly receive information enabling them to rectify any error or omission in subsequent editions. All facts are correct at time of going to press.

Published by Collins
An imprint of HarperCollins*Publishers*
1 London Bridge Street
London SE1 9GF

HarperCollins*Publishers*
Macken House, 39/40 Mayor Street Upper,
Dublin 1, D01 C9W8, Ireland

© HarperCollins*Publishers* Limited 2019
ISBN 9780008321468
First published 2019
This edition published 2022
10 9 8 7 6 5 4 3

British Library Cataloguing in Publication Data.

A CIP record of this book is available from the British Library.

Commissioning Editor: Kerry Ferguson
Project Leader and Management: Katie Galloway
Authors: Mike Smith, Sunetra Berry, Lynn Pharaoh, Kath Skillern and Paul Lewis
Cover Design: Sarah Duxbury and Kevin Robbins
Inside Concept Design: Ian Wrigley
Text Design and Layout: QBS Learning
Production: Karen Nulty
Printed by Ashford Colour Ltd

FSC
www.fsc.org
MIX
Paper
FSC™ C007454

Collins

AQA
GCSE
Combined Science: Trilogy   F
SET A – Biology: Paper 1 Foundation Tier
Author: Mike Smith

Materials   Time allowed: 1 hour 15 minutes

> **For this paper you must have:**
> - a ruler
> - a calculator.

Instructions

- Answer **all** questions in the spaces provided.
- Do all rough work in this book. Cross through any work you do not want to be marked.

Information

- There are 70 marks available on this paper.
- The marks for questions are shown in brackets.
- You are expected to use a calculator where appropriate.
- You are reminded of the need for good English and clear presentation in your answers.
- When answering questions 06.3 and 08.3 you need to make sure that your answer:
  - is clear, logical, sensibly structured
  - fully meets the requirements of the question
  - shows that each separate point or step supports the overall answer.

Advice

- In all calculations, show clearly how you work out your answer.

Name: ....

---

01   **Figure 1.1** shows four types of cell.

Figure 1.1

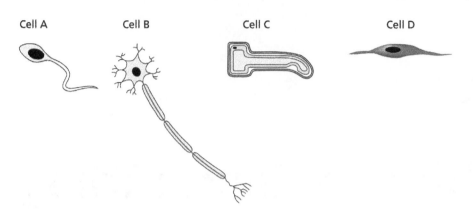

Cell A   Cell B   Cell C   Cell D

01.1 Which cell is a nerve cell?

Give **one** reason for your answer.

Cell ....

Reason ....

[2 marks]

01.2 Which cell is a root hair cell?

Give **one** reason for your answer.

Cell ....

Reason ....

[2 marks]

01.3 Which cell is a sperm cell?

Give **one** reason for your answer.

Cell ....

Reason ....

[2 marks]

01.4 Which cell comes from a plant?

Give **one** reason for your answer.

Cell ....

Reason ....

[2 marks]

Turn over >

02   Plants make glucose when they photosynthesise.

02.1 Which of the following is **not** used for photosynthesis?

Tick **one** box.

Carbon dioxide   ☐

Light   ☐

Oxygen   ☐

Water   ☐

[1 mark]

02.2 Where does most photosynthesis take place in a plant?

Tick **one** box.

Epidermal tissue   ☐

Palisade mesophyll   ☐

Phloem   ☐

Xylem   ☐

[1 mark]

02.3 What is the chemical symbol for glucose?

Tick **one** box.

$C_6H_6O_{12}$ ☐

$C_6H_{12}O_6$ ☐

$C_{12}H_6O_6$ ☐

$C_{12}H_6O_{12}$ ☐

[1 mark]

02.4 Plants can convert glucose to other substances.

Draw **one** line from each substance to its use.

Substance made from glucose		Use
Amino acids		Food storage
Cellulose		Protein synthesis
Starch		Strengthen cell walls

[2 marks]

02.5 Some of the glucose made in photosynthesis is converted to other sugars.

Use words from the box to complete the sentences.

active transport	osmosis	phloem
spongy mesophyll	translocation	xylem

Sugars are transported from the leaves to other parts of the plant through the

_____ .

This movement of sugars is called _____ .

[2 marks]

Question 2 continues on the next page

02.6 At which time of day do plants photosynthesise most?

Tick **one** box.

Midnight ☐

Early morning ☐

Midday ☐

Early evening ☐

Give **two** reasons for your answer.

1. ....

2. ....

[3 marks]

03   The blood system is made of different parts.

03.1   Draw **one** line from each part of the blood to its function.

Part of the blood	Function

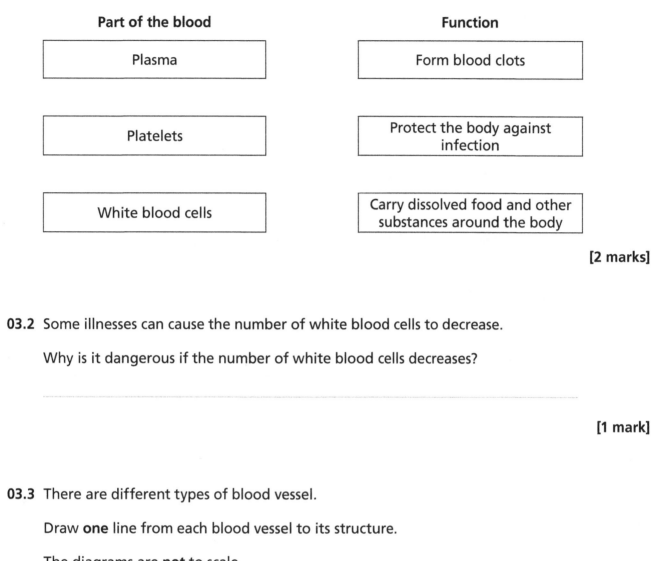

[2 marks]

03.2   Some illnesses can cause the number of white blood cells to decrease.

Why is it dangerous if the number of white blood cells decreases?

....

[1 mark]

03.3   There are different types of blood vessel.

Draw **one** line from each blood vessel to its structure.

The diagrams are **not** to scale.

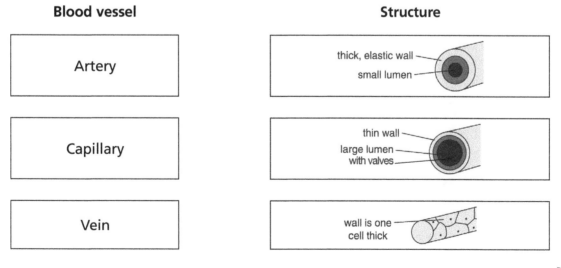

[2 marks]

Question 3 continues on the next page

03.4 In coronary heart disease there is **reduced** blood flow to the heart muscle.

Explain why it is dangerous if there is **reduced** blood flow to the heart muscle.

....

....

....

[2 marks]

03.5 Treatments for coronary heart disease include the following:

Artificial heart	**Drug treatment**	**Replacement heart valve**	**Stent**

A patient has suffered heart failure, but no suitable donor is available.

Which of these treatments should the patient have?

Explain your answer.

Treatment ....

Reason ....

....

[2 marks]

04   Malaria is a disease caused by a single-celled pathogen called *Plasmodium*.

Mosquitoes take in *Plasmodium* when they feed on an infected person.

They can then pass on *Plasmodium* to the next person they feed on.

04.1 **Figure 4.1** shows the life cycle of mosquitoes.

Mosquitoes lay their eggs in still water.

Figure 4.1

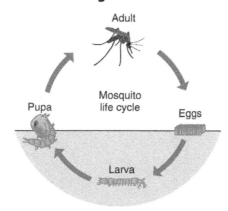

Suggest how **both** of the following help control the spread of malaria.

1. Spraying still water with oil to cover the surface.

_____

_____

2. Wearing long sleeves and long trousers.

_____

_____

[2 marks]

Question 4 continues on the next page

04.2 A type of mosquito that can spread malaria lives in the UK.

However, malaria is rare in the UK.

Suggest why these mosquitoes do **not** usually spread malaria in the UK.

_____

_____

_____

[2 marks]

04.3 Other diseases are caused by different types of pathogen.

Draw **one** line from each disease to the type of pathogen that causes it.

Disease	Type of pathogen
Measles	Bacterial
Rose black spot	Fungal
Salmonella food poisoning	Viral

[2 marks]

04.4 **Figure 4.2** shows a *Plasmodium* cell.

Figure 4.2

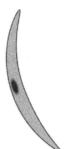

Plasmodium is a protist. It is bigger than a bacterial cell.

Give **two other** ways it is different from a bacterial cell.

1. ....

2. ....

[2 marks]

Turn over >

05   Yeast is used in the production of alcoholic drinks.

Yeast converts glucose to ethanol (alcohol) during anaerobic respiration.

05.1 What is another word for anaerobic respiration in yeast?

Tick **one** box.

Differentiation ☐

Diffusion ☐

Fermentation ☐

Ventilation ☐

[1 mark]

05.2 Figure 5.1 shows a container used to make beer.

Figure 5.1

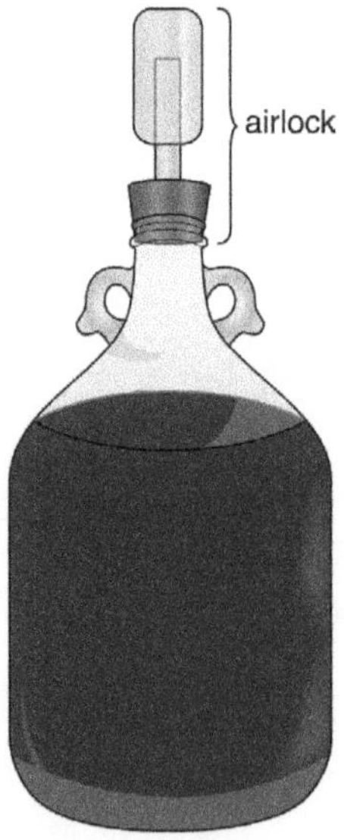

The airlock prevents any gases entering the container.

Suggest why this is necessary.

_____

_____

_____

[2 marks]

05.3 The airlock does allow gases to leave the container.

Suggest why this is necessary.

....

....

....

[2 marks]

05.4 Write the word equation for anaerobic respiration in **human muscles**.

....

[2 marks]

05.5 Humans do **not** just use anaerobic respiration.

They mainly use aerobic respiration.

Give **one** reason why humans do **not** just use anaerobic respiration.

....

....

[1 mark]

Turn over >

06   Many diseases can be treated with medicines.

06.1 The common cold is caused by a virus.

Doctors give medicines like aspirin to patients with a cold.

Doctors do **not** give antibiotics to patients with a cold.

Explain why patients with a cold should take a medicine like aspirin.

....

....

Explain why patients with a cold should **not** take antibiotics.

....

....

[2 marks]

06.2 New medicines have to be tested in clinical trials before they can be used for the general public.

Give **two** reasons why new drugs have to be tested.

1. ....

....

2. ....

....

[2 marks]

   ©HarperCollins*Publishers* 2019

06.3 Some clinical trials of new medicines use healthy volunteers, and some use ill patients.

Many clinical trials involve the use of placebos.

Should you use placebos with both healthy volunteers and ill patients?

Explain your answer.

_____

_____

_____

_____

_____

_____

_____

[4 marks]

06.4 Some clinical trials are double blind trials.

Why are double blind trials used?

_____

_____

[1 mark]

07 Microscopes can be used to study very small structures.

07.1 Figure 7.1 shows some structures of different sizes.

The diagrams are **not** to scale.

Figure 7.1

2 cm	7 μm	100 nm	3 mm
acorn	red blood cell	virus	ant

Write the objects in order of their size, from the smallest to the largest.

Smallest ....

....

....

Largest ....

[2 marks]

07.2 **Figure 7.2** shows an image of a white blood cell.

Figure 7.2

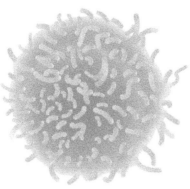

The actual diameter of the cell is 12 μm.

The diameter of the image is 60 mm.

Calculate the magnification of the image.

Use the formula:

$$\text{magnification} = \frac{\text{size of image}}{\text{size of real object}}$$

....

....

....

....

Magnification: ....

[3 marks]

07.3 When using a microscope to view cells:

- often a stain is used
- the cells are first viewed using low power.

Explain the reason for each of these.

Reason for using a stain: ....

....

Reason for viewing first with low power: ....

....

[2 marks]

Turn over >

08   **Figure 8.1** shows the apparatus that a student used to investigate transpiration.

Figure 8.1

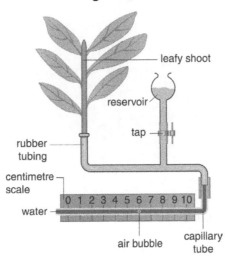

Table 8.1 shows the student's results.

Table 8.1

Time in min	Distance air bubble moved in mm
0	0
5	18
10	25
15	54
20	72

08.1 Plot the data from **Table 8.1** onto **Figure 8.2**.

Circle any anomalous results.

Draw a line of best fit.

Figure 8.2

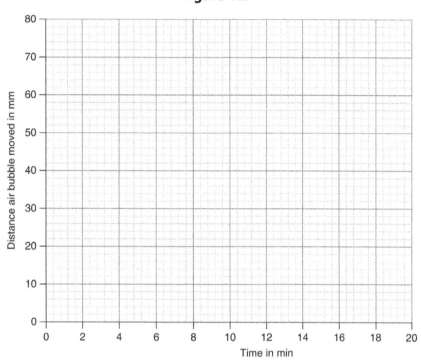

[4 marks]

08.2 Explain why transpiration caused the air bubble to move.

....

....

[1 mark]

Question 8 continues on the next page

08.3 The rate of transpiration is affected by air movement.

Describe a method you could use to investigate this.

Include the apparatus shown in **Figure 8.1**, plus an electric fan to produce air movement.

You should include:

- what you would measure
- variables you would control.

....

....

....

....

....

....

....

....

....

....

....

[6 marks]

END OF QUESTIONS

Collins

AQA

GCSE

Combined Science: Trilogy　F

SET A – Biology: Paper 2 Foundation Tier

Author: Mike Smith

Materials

Time allowed: 1 hour 15 minutes

For this paper you must have:
- a ruler
- a calculator.

Instructions

- Answer **all** questions in the spaces provided.
- Do all rough work in this book. Cross through any work you do not want to be marked.

Information

- There are 70 marks available on this paper.
- The marks for questions are shown in brackets.
- You are expected to use a calculator where appropriate.
- You are reminded of the need for good English and clear presentation in your answers.
- When answering questions 07.4 and 08.1 you need to make sure that your answer:
  - is clear, logical, sensibly structured
  - fully meets the requirements of the question
  - shows that each separate point or step supports the overall answer.

Advice

- In all calculations, show clearly how you work out your answer.

Name: _____

01 **Figure 1.1** shows some of the human hormone glands.

Figure 1.1

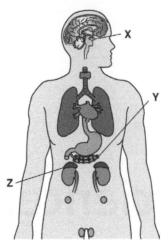

01.1 Write down the names of glands **X**, **Y** and **Z**.

Choose your answers from the list.

Adrenal

Pancreas

Pituitary

Testes

Thyroid

Gland **X**: ....

Gland **Y**: ....

Gland **Z**: ....

[3 marks]

01.2 How do hormones travel around the body?

....

[1 mark]

01.3 Draw **one** line from each hormone to the gland that secretes it.

Hormone	Gland
Insulin	Ovary
Oestrogen	Testis
Testosterone	Pancreas

[2 marks]

01.4 What health condition is caused by a lack of insulin?

_____

[1 mark]

Turn over >

02   **Figure 2.1** shows part of an Arctic food web.

Figure 2.1

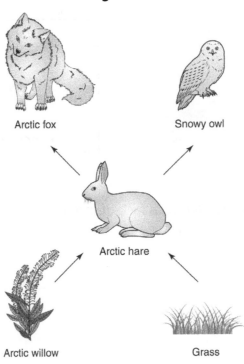

02.1 Write down **one** producer from **Figure 2.1**.

....

[1 mark]

02.2 Write down **one** secondary consumer from **Figure 2.1**.

....

[1 mark]

02.3 If the number of Arctic foxes decreased, what would start to happen to the number of snowy owls?

Give a reason for your answer.

Answer: ....

Reason: ....

....

[2 marks]

02.4 What term describes all the organisms in the Arctic food web?

Tick **one** box.

Community ☐

Ecosystem ☐

Environment ☐

Habitat ☐

[1 mark]

02.5 Some organisms in the Arctic food web may compete for **biotic** factors.

Which factor can be described as biotic?

Tick **one** box.

Light ☐

Mates ☐

Mineral ions ☐

Water ☐

[1 mark]

Question 2 continues on the next page

02.6 **Figure 2.2** shows an Arctic fox.

Figure 2.2

Arctic foxes are predators.

Identify **one** adaptation that helps an Arctic fox survive as a predator.

Explain how the adaptation helps it survive.

Adaptation: _____

How it helps survival as a predator: _____

_____

[2 marks]

02.7 **Figure 2.3** shows an Arctic hare.

Figure 2.3

Arctic hares are prey animals.

Identify **one** adaptation that helps an Arctic hare survive as a prey animal.

Explain how the adaptation helps it survive.

Adaptation: _____

How it helps survival as a prey animal: _____

_____

[2 marks]

03 Hormones are involved in human reproduction.

03.1 Draw **one** line from each hormone to its function.

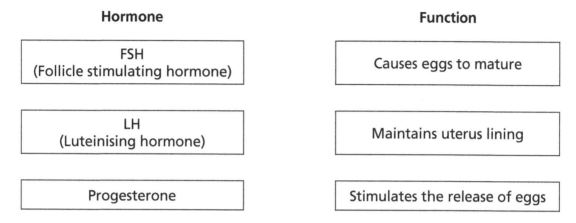

Hormone

FSH
(Follicle stimulating hormone)

LH
(Luteinising hormone)

Progesterone

Function

Causes eggs to mature

Maintains uterus lining

Stimulates the release of eggs

[2 marks]

03.2 Complete **Table 3.1** to show the number of chromosomes in the different types of human cell.

Table 3.1

Type of cell	Number of chromosomes in cell
Sperm	
Egg	
Fertilised egg	46
Embryo	

[2 marks]

Question 3 continues on the next page

03.3 As an embryo grows, different types of cells develop.

What is this process called?

Tick **one** box.

Differentiation ☐

Fusion ☐

Meiosis ☐

Reproduction ☐

[1 mark]

03.4 Draw **one** line from each contraceptive to how it works.

Contraceptive	How it works
Diaphragm	Kills sperm
Intrauterine device (IUD)	Prevents eggs maturing
Oral contraceptive	Prevents fertilised egg implanting
Spermicide	Prevents sperm reaching egg

[3 marks]

04 **Figure 4.1** shows carbon dioxide emissions in California.

Pie chart **B** shows the breakdown of the emissions from transportation.

Figure 4.1

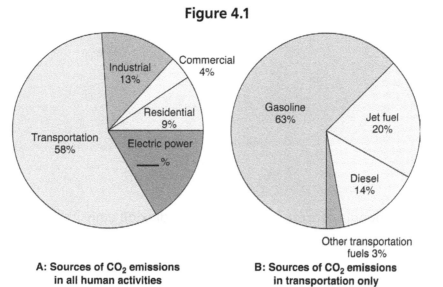

A: Sources of CO$_2$ emissions
in all human activities

B: Sources of CO$_2$ emissions
in transportation only

04.1 Calculate the percentage of carbon dioxide emissions from electric power.

....

....

....

Answer = ... %

[2 marks]

04.2 Why does using electric power cause carbon dioxide emissions?

....

....

[2 marks]

Question 4 continues on the next page

04.3 Which produces more carbon dioxide emissions, industrial activities **or** jet fuel?

Show your working out to justify your answer.

....

....

....

....

[2 marks]

04.4 Why are many people concerned about carbon dioxide emissions?

....

....

[1 mark]

04.5 Which process **removes** carbon dioxide from the atmosphere?

Tick **one** box.

Combustion ☐

Deforestation ☐

Photosynthesis ☐

Respiration ☐

[1 mark]

©HarperCollins*Publishers* 2019

05   Variation is caused by the environment or genes.

Figure 5.1 shows some human features that show variation.

Figure 5.1

05.1 Identify **one** feature from **Figure 5.1** that is caused by the environment.

....

[1 mark]

05.2 Use words from the box to complete the sentences.

chromosome	DNA	double helix
genome	polymer	protein	strand

Genes are made of a chemical called ...., which forms a shape

called a ....

Genes are small sections of a structure called a ....

[3 marks]

Question 5 continues on the next page

05.3 Earwax can be either wet or dry.

Two alleles control this:

- wet (**A**)
- dry (**a**)

The wet allele is dominant to the dry allele.

Figure 5.2 shows a genetic cross between two people, each with the genotype **Aa**.

Complete **Figure 5.2**.

Figure 5.2

	A	a
A		Aa
a		

[2 marks]

05.4 What is the **phenotype** of someone with the genotype **Aa**?

....

[1 mark]

05.5 Which term describes someone with the genotype **Aa**?

Tick **one** box.

Dominant ☐

Heterozygous ☐

Homozygous ☐

Recessive ☐

[1 mark]

06   **Figure 6.1** shows a modern breed of cow and a wild cow.

Modern breeds of cow were produced by selective breeding starting with wild cows similar to that shown in **Figure 6.1**.

Figure 6.1

Wild cow   Modern breed of cow

06.1 The modern breed of cow has more meat than the wild cow.

Describe how selective breeding can produce a cow with more meat.

....

....

....

....

....

....

....

....

....

[5 marks]

Question 6 continues on the next page

06.2 Identify **one other** feature in **Figure 6.1** that has been selectively bred for.

Explain why the feature has been selectively bred for.

Feature: ....

Reason: ....

....

[2 marks]

06.3 Some plant crops have been selectively bred.

Other plant crops have been changed by introducing genes from other species.

What is this process called?

Tick **one** box.

Genetic cross ☐

Genetic engineering ☐

Genetic mutation ☐

Genetic variation ☐

[1 mark]

07   In a park, some grassland is left to grow wild except for a path which is mown regularly.

Students used a transect line to investigate how the path affected the distribution of four different plant species.

Figure 7.1 shows the line of the transect.

The students placed quadrats every metre along the transect.

Figure 7.1

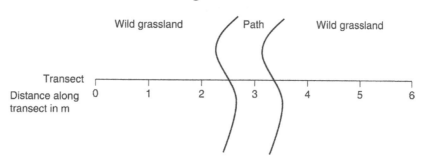

Table 7.1 shows their results.

Table 7.1

Distance along transect in m		0	1	2	3	4	5	6
Number of individual plants of each species per quadrat	Species A	5	4	3	0	4	6	5
	Species B	0	0	1	8	2	0	0
	Species C	4	3	2	0	3	4	4
	Species D	0	0	2	3	1	0	0

07.1 Look at **Table 7.1**.

What is the mode number per quadrat for species D?

Answer: _____

[1 mark]

Question 7 continues on the next page

07.2 Look at **Table 7.1**.

What is the median number per quadrat for species A?

Answer: _____

[1 mark]

07.3 **Figure 7.2** shows kite diagrams of the results.

Use the data for **species A** from **Table 7.1** to complete **Figure 7.2**.

Figure 7.2

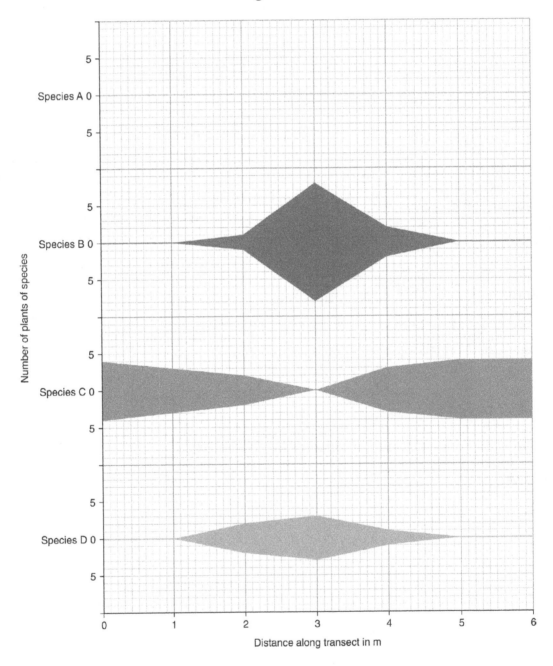

[4 marks]

07.4 **Figure 7.3** shows pictures of each plant species.

Figure 7.3

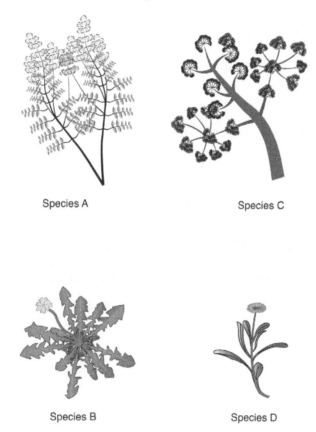

Species A

Species C

Species B

Species D

Suggest reasons for the distributions of the four species along the transect.

Use information from **Table 7.1** and **Figures 7.1**, **7.2** and **7.3** to help you answer.

....

....

....

....

....

....

....

....

[4 marks]

Turn over >

08 A group of students investigated their reaction times.

They each took it in turn to press a timer button as soon as they heard a buzzer.

Each student used their right hand.

Each student took the test three times and recorded their shortest reaction time.

There were eight girls and six boys in the group.

Table 8.1 shows their results.

Table 8.1

	Shortest reaction times in s								Mean reaction time in s
Girls	0.21	0.16	0.18	0.19	0.18	0.16	0.20	0.19	0.18
Boys	0.19	0.15	0.32	0.16	0.17	0.20			0.20

08.1 One of the students made this conclusion:

Girls have shorter reaction times than boys.

Evaluate the method used and the student's conclusion.

....

....

....

....

....

....

....

....

....

....

[6 marks]

08.2 **Figure 8.1** shows the nerve pathway involved in the investigation.

Figure 8.1

Sound of buzzer ⟶ Ear ⟶ Brain ⟶ Hand muscles ⟶ Press button

In **Figure 8.1**, which is the receptor and which is the effector?

Receptor: ....

Effector: ....

[2 marks]

Question 8 continues on the next page

08.3 How does information pass along a nerve pathway?

_____

_____

[2 marks]

08.4 One of the students says:

Pressing the button quickly is an example of a reflex action.

Is the student correct?

Give a reason for your answer.

Is the student correct? _____

Reason: _____

_____

[1 mark]

END OF QUESTIONS

Collins

AQA
GCSE
Combined Science: Trilogy   F
SET A – Chemistry: Paper 3 Foundation Tier

Author: Sunetra Berry

Materials   Time allowed: 1 hour 15 minutes

For this paper you must have:

- a ruler
- a calculator
- the Periodic Table (found at the end of the paper).

Instructions

- Answer all questions in the spaces provided.
- Do all rough work in this book. Cross through any work you do not want to be marked.

Information

- There are 70 marks available on this paper.
- The marks for questions are shown in brackets.
- You are expected to use a calculator where appropriate.
- You are reminded of the need for good English and clear presentation in your answers.
- When answering questions 03.5 and 05.1 you need to make sure that your answer:
  - is clear, logical, sensibly structured
  - fully meets the requirements of the question
  - shows that each separate point or step supports the overall answer.

Advice

- In all calculations, show clearly how you work out your answer.

Name: _____

01   This question is about atoms, elements, mixtures and compounds.

01.1 Which **one** of the following is an **element**?

Tick **one** box.

H_2O ☐

O_2 ☐

Fe_3O_4 ☐

HCl   ☐   [1 mark]

01.2 Which of these statements is **true**?

Tick **one** box.

All atoms have an equal number of protons and neutrons.   ☐

All atoms have an equal number of protons and electrons.   ☐

All atoms have an equal number of protons, neutrons and electrons. ☐

All atoms have a different number of protons and neutrons.   ☐

[1 mark]

01.3 Which diagram shows the correct electronic structure for the ion of magnesium, Mg^{2+}?

The atomic number of magnesium is 12.

Tick **one** box.

[1 mark]

01.4 A student wants to separate **soluble** sodium chloride from **insoluble** calcium carbonate.

Which of the following lists the steps in the correct order?

Tick **one** box.

Add water, heat, cool to crystallise, and filter. ☐

Add water, filter, heat, and cool to crystallise. ☐

Add water, heat, filter, and cool to crystallise. ☐

Add water, filter, cool to crystallise, and heat. ☐

[1 mark]

Question 1 continues on the next page

01.5 Which statement about the formulae for the four different compounds below is **true**?

Tick **one** box.

$Ca(OH)_2$ has two calcium atoms. ☐

$Ca(HCO_3)_2$ has two carbon atoms. ☐

$Al(NO_3)_3$ has six oxygen atoms. ☐

$(NH_4)_2SO_4$ has six hydrogen atoms. ☐

[1 mark]

01.6 An atom of one of the elements forms ions with an electronic structure 2,8,8

It does this by losing two electrons.

Which element is it?

[1 mark]

01.7 On the Periodic Table, the symbol of sodium, Na, is shown as:

$$^{23}_{11}Na$$

Use this to write down **three** pieces of information about the numbers of different particles in a sodium atom.

[3 marks]

02.1 Draw a diagram to show the arrangement of particles in a **liquid**.

Use the box below.

[2 marks]

02.2 Table 1.1 shows data about the melting and boiling points of different substances.

Table 1.1

Substance	Melting point (°C)	Boiling point (°C)
water	0	100
silver chloride	455	1557
sulfur dioxide	−75	−10
sodium chloride	808	1465
oxygen	−219	−183

Which **two** of the following statements are **true**?

Tick **two** boxes.

Water has the lowest melting point. ☐

At 1500°C, silver chloride is a liquid. ☐

Oxygen has the lowest melting point. ☐

Silver chloride has the highest melting point. ☐

[2 marks]

02.3 Which two substances from **Table 1.1** are **ionically bonded**?

Use the information about their melting points and boiling points to help you.

1. _____

2. _____

[2 marks]

Turn over >

03

03.1 What is the name given to a chemical reaction in which energy is **released**?

....

[1 mark]

03.2 What type of reaction is shown in **Figure 3.1**?

Figure 3.1

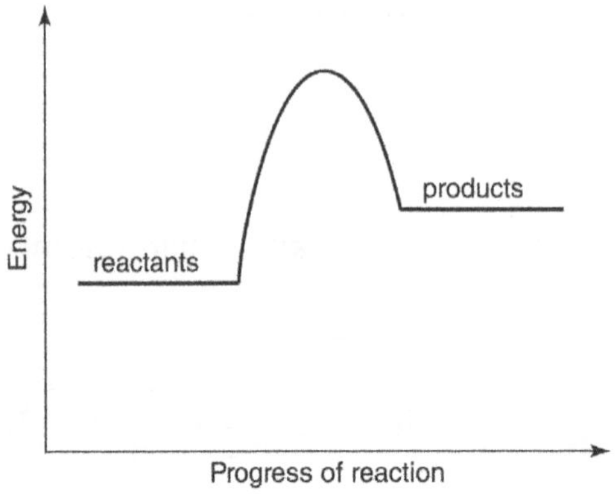

Type of reaction: ....

[1 mark]

03.3 Give **two** examples of useful endothermic reactions.

1. ....

2. ....

[2 marks]

03.4 In an experiment, four different metals were placed in hydrochloric acid.

The temperature changes of the reactions were measured.

Table 3.1 shows the results.

Table 3.1

Metal	Temperature change (°C)
copper	0
iron	2
magnesium	15
aluminium	8

Write the metals in order of their reactivity, with **the most reactive first**.

Explain how these results led to your answer.

....

....

....

....

....

....

[3 marks]

Question 3 continues on the next page

03.5 Describe how the experiment might be safely carried out to obtain the data in **Table 3.1**.

Describe:

- which measurements should be made, and how they should be made

- how to make the experiment fair

- how to obtain accurate, precise data.

[6 marks]

04   Salts are produced by neutralising of acids using insoluble bases.

04.1 Complete the word equation for the reaction of sulfuric acid and copper oxide.

sulfuric acid + copper oxide → .... + water

[1 mark]

04.2 Copper oxide is an insoluble solid.

The salt produced by the reaction of sulfuric acid and copper oxide is soluble.

How can you tell when all the acid has been neutralised?

....

....

[1 mark]

04.3 Calcium chloride is produced by the reaction of calcium carbonate with hydrochloric acid.

Balance the equation for the reaction by writing the correct number in the box below.

$CaCO_3(s) +$ ☐ $HCl(aq) \rightarrow CaCl_2(aq) + H_2O(l) + CO_2(g)$

[1 mark]

04.4 Look at the state symbols in the equation above.

What would **appear** to happen to the mass of the reactants during the course of the reaction?

....

....

[1 mark]

Question 4 continues on the next page

04.5 A student carried out the reaction of calcium carbonate with excess hydrochloric acid.

He measured the mass of calcium chloride crystals made using different amounts of calcium carbonate.

Table 4.1 shows the student's results.

Table 4.1

Mass of calcium carbonate (g)	Mass of calcium chloride crystals made (g)
10	11.0
20	22.0
30	28.0
40	
50	55.0
60	66.0

Plot these results on the grid below.

Circle any anomalous results.

Draw a line of best fit.

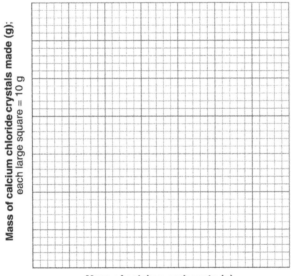

Mass of calcium carbonate (g); each large square = 10 g

[3 marks]

04.6 Use your graph to predict the amount of calcium chloride formed from 40 g of calcium carbonate.

Describe the pattern of your graph.

Amount of calcium chloride = _____ g

Pattern of graph: _____

_____

[2 marks]

04.7 If the total mass of calcium carbonate and hydrochloric acid was 136.5 g, what would you expect the total mass of **all** the products to be?

Explain your answer.

_____

_____

_____

[2 marks]

04.8 Hydrochloric acid is made of hydrogen chloride dissolved in water.

The concentration of hydrochloric acid used here is 20 g/dm³.

Calculate how many grams of hydrogen chloride are needed to make up this concentration of hydrochloric acid in 250 cm³ of solution.

1 dm³ = 1000 cm³.

_____

_____

_____

[2 marks]

Question 4 continues on the next page

04.9 The student then reacted nitric acid with calcium carbonate, instead of hydrochloric acid.

Use **Table 4.2** to work out the name and formula of the new salt made.

Table 4.2

Common ion	Formula
chloride	Cl^-
sulfate	SO_4^{2-}
nitrate	NO_3
calcium	Ca^{2+}
carbonate	CO_3^{2-}

[2 marks]

Name: ....

Formula: ....

05.1 Metals can be extracted from their ores using these methods:

- electrolysis of molten ore

- reduction with carbon

- no processing needed.

Gold is found in the Earth as pure gold. Iron is found as iron oxide.Sodium is found as sodium chloride.

Compare the methods of extracting gold, iron and sodium from their ores.

Include in your answer:

- how the reactivity of each metal affects the method of extraction

- word equations where appropriate.

_____

_____

_____

_____

_____

_____

_____

_____

_____

_____

[6 marks]

Turn over >

06 This question is about bonding and structure.

06.1 Which of the following structures does **not** have weak intermolecular forces?

Tick **one** box.

 ☐

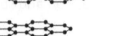 ☐

 ☐

 ☐

[1 mark]

06.2 The formation of sodium chloride, NaCl, can be represented by this equation.

$$Na\bullet + {}^{x}_{x}\overset{xx}{\underset{xx}{Cl}}{}^{x}_{x} \longrightarrow [Na]^{+} \left[{}^{x}_{x}\overset{xx}{\underset{xx}{Cl}}{}^{x}_{x} \right]$$
(2, 8, 1) (2, 8, 7)   (2, 8) (2, 8, 8)

Write a similar equation to show the formation of magnesium fluoride, MgF_2

[2 marks]

06.3 Which one of the following structures of carbon does **not** conduct electricity?

Tick **one** box.

☐

☐

☐

☐

[1 mark]

06.4 List the main differences between **small** covalent compounds and **giant** covalent compounds, and their properties.

_____

_____

_____

_____

_____

[3 marks]

Turn over >

07

07.1 Which of the elements in Group 7 has the highest boiling **and** melting point?

Tick **one** box.

Bromine ☐

Chlorine ☐

Fluorine ☐

Iodine ☐

[1 mark]

07.2 Draw a dot and cross diagram to show the bonding in a fluorine molecule. The atomic number for fluorine is 9.

Show the outer most electrons only.

\
\
\
\
\
\
\

[2 marks]

07.3 Group 1 elements react with water.

Describe:

- observations you would see in reactions between Group 1 elements and water

- the way the reactivity changes down Group 1.

Group 7 elements react with dissolved salts of less reactive halogens.

Describe:

- observations you would see in reactions between Group 7 elements and dissolved salts of less reactive halogens

- the way the reactivity changes down Group 7.

....

....

....

....

....

....

[4 marks]

Turn over >

08.1 The electrolysis cell shown in **Figure 8.1** contains an electrolyte of molten sodium iodide.

The two electrodes are unreactive.

Figure 8.1

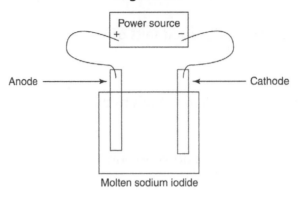

Molten sodium iodide

Which statement is **true**?

Tick **one** box.

Sodium is formed at the anode. ☐

Iodine is formed at the anode. ☐

Hydrogen is formed at the cathode. ☐

Hydrogen is formed at the anode. ☐

[1 mark]

08.2 Explain why magnesium, sodium and potassium must be extracted from their ores using electrolysis, and not using other methods.

....

....

....

....

[2 marks]

08.3 Describe what you would observe in the electrolysis of **aqueous copper chloride**.

Explain these observations.

Name the products formed at each electrode.

_____

_____

_____

_____

_____

_____

_____

_____

_____

_____

_____

_____

[4 marks]

END OF QUESTIONS

The Periodic Table

Key
- Metals
- Non-metals

Key to element box:
- Relative atomic mass
- Atomic symbol
- Name
- Atomic/proton number

Example:
1 / H / hydrogen / 1

1	2												3	4	5	6	7	0 or 8
																		4 **He** helium 2
7 **Li** lithium 3	9 **Be** beryllium 4												11 **B** boron 5	12 **C** carbon 6	14 **N** nitrogen 7	16 **O** oxygen 8	19 **F** fluorine 9	20 **Ne** neon 10
23 **Na** sodium 11	24 **Mg** magnesium 12												27 **Al** aluminium 13	28 **Si** silicon 14	31 **P** phosphorus 15	32 **S** sulfur 16	35.5 **Cl** chlorine 17	40 **Ar** argon 18
39 **K** potassium 19	40 **Ca** calcium 20	45 **Sc** scandium 21	48 **Ti** titanium 22	51 **V** vanadium 23	52 **Cr** chromium 24	55 **Mn** manganese 25	56 **Fe** iron 26	59 **Co** cobalt 27	59 **Ni** nickel 28	63.5 **Cu** copper 29	65 **Zn** zinc 30		70 **Ga** gallium 31	73 **Ge** germanium 32	75 **As** arsenic 33	79 **Se** selenium 34	80 **Br** bromine 35	84 **Kr** krypton 36
85 **Rb** rubidium 37	88 **Sr** strontium 38	89 **Y** yttrium 39	91 **Zr** zirconium 40	93 **Nb** niobium 41	96 **Mo** molybdenum 42	[98] **Tc** technetium 43	101 **Ru** ruthenium 44	103 **Rh** rhodium 45	106 **Pd** palladium 46	108 **Ag** silver 47	112 **Cd** cadmium 48		115 **In** indium 49	119 **Sn** tin 50	122 **Sb** antimony 51	128 **Te** tellurium 52	127 **I** iodine 53	131 **Xe** xenon 54
133 **Cs** caesium 55	137 **Ba** barium 56	139 **La*** lanthanum 57	178 **Hf** hafnium 72	181 **Ta** tantalum 73	184 **W** tungsten 74	186 **Re** rhenium 75	190 **Os** osmium 76	192 **Ir** iridium 77	195 **Pt** platinum 78	197 **Au** gold 79	201 **Hg** mercury 80		204 **Tl** thallium 81	207 **Pb** lead 82	209 **Bi** bismuth 83	[209] **Po** polonium 84	[210] **At** astatine 85	[222] **Rn** radon 86
[223] **Fr** francium 87	[226] **Ra** radium 88	[227] **Ac*** actinium 89	[261] **Rf** rutherfordium 104	[262] **Db** dubnium 105	[266] **Sg** seaborgium 106	[264] **Bh** bohrium 107	[277] **Hs** hassium 108	[268] **Mt** meitnerium 109	[271] **Ds** darmstadtium 110	[272] **Rg** roentgenium 111	[285] **Cn** copernicium 112		[286] **Uut** ununtrium 113	[289] **Fl** flerovium 114	[289] **Uup** ununpentium 115	[293] **Lv** livermorium 116	[294] **Uus** ununseptium 117	[294] **Uuo** ununoctium 118

*The lanthanides (atomic numbers 58–71) and the actinides (atomic numbers 90–103) have been omitted.

The relative atomic masses of copper and chlorine have not been rounded to the nearest whole number.

Collins

AQA

GCSE

Combined Science: Trilogy   F

SET A – Chemistry: Paper 4 Foundation Tier

Author: Sunetra Berry

Materials   Time allowed: 1 hour 15 minutes

For this paper you must have:

- a ruler
- a calculator
- the Periodic Table (found at the end of the paper).

Instructions

- Answer all questions in the spaces provided.
- Do all rough work in this book. Cross through any work you do not want to be marked.

Information

- There are 70 marks available on this paper.
- The marks for questions are shown in brackets.
- You are expected to use a calculator where appropriate.
- You are reminded of the need for good English and clear presentation in your answers.
- When answering question 03.3 you need to make sure that your answer:
  - is clear, logical, sensibly structured
  - fully meets the requirements of the question
  - shows that each separate point or step supports the overall answer.

Advice

- In all calculations, show clearly how you work out your answer.

Name: ....

---

01   This question is about oxygen and the other gases that make up the atmosphere.

01.1   Which of the statements below is a test of an unknown gas for oxygen?

Tick **one** box.

A lighted splint goes 'pop'. ☐

Limewater goes cloudy when the gas is bubbled through it. ☐

Blue litmus paper turns white when held in the gas. ☐

A glowing splint relights when held in the gas. ☐

[1 mark]

01.2   Which gas was the most abundant in the Earth's early atmosphere?

Tick **one** box.

Carbon dioxide ☐

Nitrogen ☐

Ammonia ☐

Oxygen ☐

[1 mark]

01.3   Which **two** gases are the most abundant in the Earth's atmosphere today?

Tick **two** boxes.

Carbon dioxide ☐

Nitrogen ☐

Ammonia ☐

Oxygen ☐

[2 marks]

01.4 Complete the sentences below about how the atmosphere has changed.

Choose words from the box below.

nitrogen	oxygen	evaporated	increased	condensed
dissolved	carbonates	nitrates	decreased	

Photosynthesis increased the amount of _____ in the atmosphere.

The levels of carbon dioxide _____ as a result of the formation of the oceans.

This is because the carbon dioxide _____ in the oceans.

Sediments and rocks were formed as a result of the production of _____ .

[4 marks]

01.5 Which statements about pure substances are correct?

Tick **two** boxes.

Air is a pure substance – it has the same composition everywhere. ☐

Distilled water is a pure substance as nothing has been added to it. ☐

A pure substance has fixed melting and boiling points. ☐

An ore is a pure substance because it occurs naturally. ☐

[2 marks]

01.6 Which two are examples of a **formulation**?

Tick **two** boxes.

Cough mixture ☐

Air ☐

Sea water ☐

Cleaning agent ☐

[2 marks]

Turn over >

02.1 **Table 2.1** shows the main sources of atmospheric pollutants and their effects on the environment.

Complete the table where it is labelled A, B, C and D.

Table 2.1

Name of pollutant	Main source of pollutant	Effect of pollutant on the environment
carbon dioxide	burning fossil fuels	A
sulfur dioxide, oxides of nitrogen	burning diesel and petrol fuels	B
C	D	global dimming

[4 marks]

03   This question is about fractional distillation of crude oil and the production of fuels.

Figure 3.1 shows a simple diagram of a fractionating column with some of the fuels it produces.

Figure 3.1

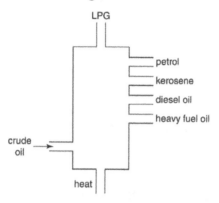

Table 3.1 gives some information about each of the fractions.

Table 3.1

Fraction	Number of carbon atoms	Boiling point (°C)
liquefied petroleum gas	1–4	
petrol	5–10	40–80
kerosene	10–16	
diesel oil	16–20	250–350
heavy fuel oil	20–79	

03.1 The boiling points of liquefied petroleum gas, kerosene and fuel oil are missing.

Choose from the following values and add them to **Table 3.1**.

above 370	20–30	150–230

[2 marks]

Question 3 continues on the next page

03.2 Explain why the boiling points are **not** fixed values but cover a range of values.

....

....

....

[2 marks]

03.3 Describe how a fractionating column works.

Include information about:

- how the size of the molecules of the crude oil fractions affects their boiling points

- evaporation of the fractions, and

- condensation of the fractions.

....

....

....

....

....

....

....

....

....

....

....

....

....

[6 marks]

  ©HarperCollins*Publishers* 2019

04.1 Which of the following structures is propane?

Tick **one** box.

[1 mark]

04.2 Complete the word equation to show the complete combustion of propane.

propane + ... → .... + water

[2 marks]

04.3 What would be different about the combustion of hexane, C_6H_{14}, when compared with the combustion of propane?

....

[1 mark]

04.4 The process of **cracking** is used to break down longer chain alkanes into shorter chain alkanes.

Balance the equation for cracking $C_{18}H_{38}$.

$$C_{18}H_{38} \rightarrow \boxed{} \ C_2H_4 + C_6H_{14}$$

[1 mark]

04.5 The process above has produced an **alkene**, C_2H_4, and an **alkane**, C_6H_{14}.

Describe a chemical test to tell alkanes and alkenes apart from each other.

Describe the result you would expect in each case.

....

....

....

....

....

....

[3 marks]
Turn over >

05.1 Below is a list of some natural and synthetic materials.

cotton	plastics	polyester	nylon	pvc	wool

Write each of them in the correct column in **Table 5.1**.

Table 5.1

Natural materials	Synthetic materials

[3 marks]

05.2 **Figure 5.1** shows data on the use of plastics over time.

Figure 5.1

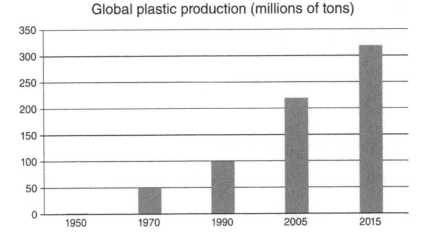

Global plastic production (millions of tons)

Describe **two** trends shown by this data.

1. ....

....

2. ....

....

[2 marks]

05.3 How would you expect the trend to continue over the **next** fifty years?

Explain your answer.

....

....

....

[2 marks]

05.4 Plastic bags are now being produced from corn starch instead of from crude oil.

Explain why corn starch is a better choice of raw material.

....

....

....

[1 mark]

Turn over >

06 **Table 6.1** shows some information about different materials.

Table 6.1

Material	Raw materials in production	Ways the material can be reused or recycled
soda-lime glass	sand, sodium carbonate, limestone	crushed and melted to make different glass products
brick	clay	crushed and used for aggregate or new bricks
concrete	limestone, sand, chippings	crushed and used for aggregate or new concrete
iron	iron ore, coke, limestone	separated and recycled to make new metal
plastics	crude oil	heated and recycled to make new objects; limited times it can be recycled

06.1 Explain why it is important to find ways to reduce the use of materials like these, or reuse or recycle them.

....

....

....

....

....

....

[3 marks]

06.2 A student claims that:

- it is better to make windows from glass than from plastic, and

- it is better to build using bricks rather than concrete.

Discuss the possible reasons for and against these statements.

Use your own knowledge and the information from **Table 6.1**.

....

....

....

....

....

....

....

....

....

....

[4 marks]

Turn over >

07

07.1 Describe the differences between **potable** water and **pure** water.

....

....

....

....

[2 marks]

07.2 Sterilisation is used to try and remove all pathogens from water.

Figure 7.1 shows the results of a study which compares three main sterilising agents: chlorine, ozone and ultraviolet.

Figure 7.1

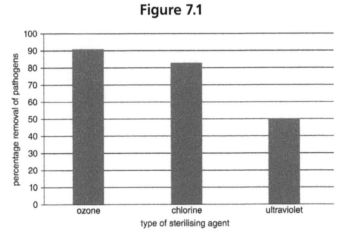

What **two** conclusions can you draw from these results?

Use data from the graph to support your answers.

1. ....

....

2. ....

....

[2 marks]

07.3 State **two** ways that the investigators could make the study a fair test.

1. ....

....

2. ....

....

[2 marks]

07.4 What is different about the **treatment of sewage**, when compared with the **treatment of ground water**?

....

....

....

....

....

....

....

....

[4 marks]

Turn over >

08

08.1 A student investigated the rate of reaction between magnesium and an acid.

The student used magnesium powder and magnesium ribbon.

The results are presented in **Figure 8.1**, but the student forgot to label the data.

Draw a line of best fit for each set of data.

Label each line of best fit as either **powder** or **ribbon**.

Figure 8.1

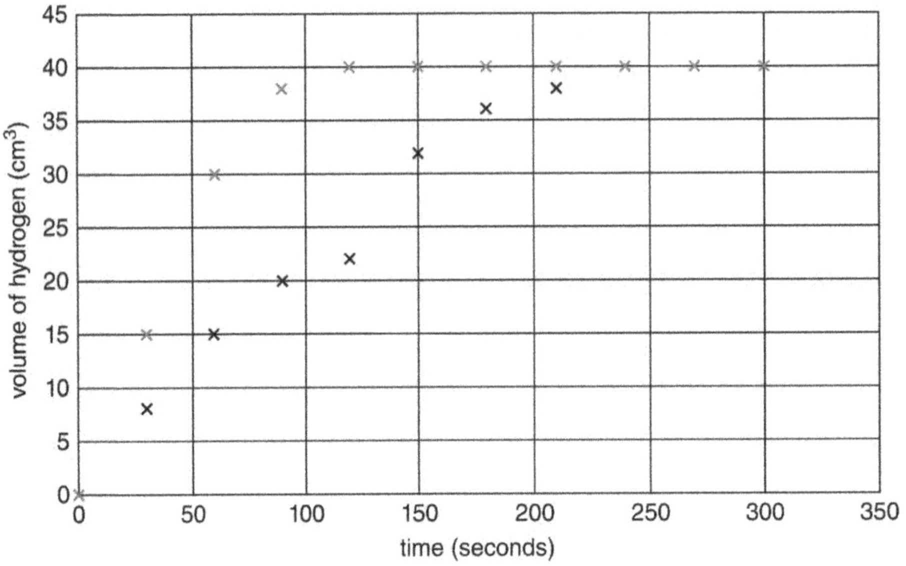

[3 marks]

08.2 Calculate the mean rate of reaction for the **powder**.

Use data from the graph.

Give your answer to 3 significant figures.

Rate = _____ cm³/s

[3 marks]

08.3 Explain why there is a difference in the rate of reaction with powder and ribbon.

Use the idea of particles in your explanation.

....

....

....

....

....

[2 marks]

08.4 The temperature of the acid is now increased by 10 °C

Explain why this will affect the rate of **both** reactions.

Use the idea of particles in your explanation.

....

....

....

....

....

[3 marks]

END OF QUESTIONS

The Periodic Table

Key

■ Metals
□ Non-metals

Relative atomic mass →	1
Atomic symbol →	**H**
Name →	hydrogen
Atomic/proton number →	1

1	2											3	4	5	6	7	0 or 8
																	4 **He** helium 2
7 **Li** lithium 3	9 **Be** beryllium 4											11 **B** boron 5	12 **C** carbon 6	14 **N** nitrogen 7	16 **O** oxygen 8	19 **F** fluorine 9	20 **Ne** neon 10
23 **Na** sodium 11	24 **Mg** magnesium 12											27 **Al** aluminium 13	28 **Si** silicon 14	31 **P** phosphorus 15	32 **S** sulfur 16	35.5 **Cl** chlorine 17	40 **Ar** argon 18
39 **K** potassium 19	40 **Ca** calcium 20	45 **Sc** scandium 21	48 **Ti** titanium 22	51 **V** vanadium 23	52 **Cr** chromium 24	55 **Mn** manganese 25	56 **Fe** iron 26	59 **Co** cobalt 27	59 **Ni** nickel 28	63.5 **Cu** copper 29	65 **Zn** zinc 30	70 **Ga** gallium 31	73 **Ge** germanium 32	75 **As** arsenic 33	79 **Se** selenium 34	80 **Br** bromine 35	84 **Kr** krypton 36
85 **Rb** rubidium 37	88 **Sr** strontium 38	89 **Y** yttrium 39	91 **Zr** zirconium 40	93 **Nb** niobium 41	96 **Mo** molybdenum 42	[98] **Tc** technetium 43	101 **Ru** ruthenium 44	103 **Rh** rhodium 45	106 **Pd** palladium 46	108 **Ag** silver 47	112 **Cd** cadmium 48	115 **In** indium 49	119 **Sn** tin 50	122 **Sb** antimony 51	128 **Te** tellurium 52	127 **I** iodine 53	131 **Xe** xenon 54
133 **Cs** caesium 55	137 **Ba** barium 56	139 **La*** lanthanum 57	178 **Hf** hafnium 72	181 **Ta** tantalum 73	184 **W** tungsten 74	186 **Re** rhenium 75	190 **Os** osmium 76	192 **Ir** iridium 77	195 **Pt** platinum 78	197 **Au** gold 79	201 **Hg** mercury 80	204 **Tl** thallium 81	207 **Pb** lead 82	209 **Bi** bismuth 83	[209] **Po** polonium 84	[210] **At** astatine 85	[222] **Rn** radon 86
[223] **Fr** francium 87	[226] **Ra** radium 88	[227] **Ac*** actinium 89	[261] **Rf** rutherfordium 104	[262] **Db** dubnium 105	[266] **Sg** seaborgium 106	[264] **Bh** bohrium 107	[277] **Hs** hassium 108	[268] **Mt** meitnerium 109	[271] **Ds** darmstadtium 110	[272] **Rg** roentgenium 111	[285] **Cn** copernicium 112	[286] **Uut** ununtrium 113	[289] **Fl** flerovium 114	[289] **Uup** ununpentium 115	[293] **Lv** livermorium 116	[294] **Uus** ununseptium 117	[294] **Uuo** ununoctium 118

*The lanthanides (atomic numbers 58–71) and the actinides (atomic numbers 90–103) have been omitted.
The relative atomic masses of copper and chlorine have not been rounded to the nearest whole number.

Collins

AQA
GCSE
Combined Science: Trilogy   F
SET A – Physics: Paper 5 Foundation Tier

Author: Lynn Pharaoh

Materials   Time allowed: 1 hour 15 minutes

For this paper you must have:

- a ruler
- a calculator
- the Physics Equation Sheet (found at the end of the paper).

Instructions

- Answer all questions in the spaces provided.
- Do all rough work in this book. Cross through any work you do not want to be marked.

Information

- There are 70 marks available on this paper.
- The marks for questions are shown in brackets.
- You are expected to use a calculator where appropriate.
- You are reminded of the need for good English and clear presentation in your answers.
- When answering questions 03.4, 05.2 and 07.2 you need to make sure that your answer:
  - is clear, logical, sensibly structured
  - fully meets the requirements of the question
  - shows that each separate point or step supports the overall answer.

Advice

- In all calculations, show clearly how you work out your answer.

Name: ....

01 In the particle model of matter, particles are sometimes shown as small circles.

01.1 Draw particles in the box to show the particle model of a **gas**.

[1 mark]

01.2 Describe the motion of the gas particles.

....

....

[2 marks]

01.3 Give the term that is used to describe the total kinetic energy and potential energy of all of the particles in a gas.

....

[1 mark]

01.4 Which **two** of the following statements correctly describe the behaviour of a gas heated at a constant volume?

Tick **two** boxes.

Increasing the temperature increases the speed of the gas particles. ☐

Increasing the temperature decreases the average kinetic energy of the particles. ☐

Increasing the temperature decreases the gas pressure. ☐

Increasing the temperature increases the gas pressure. ☐

[2 marks]

02 The circuit diagram in **Figure 2.1** shows two resistors connected to a cell.

Figure 2.1

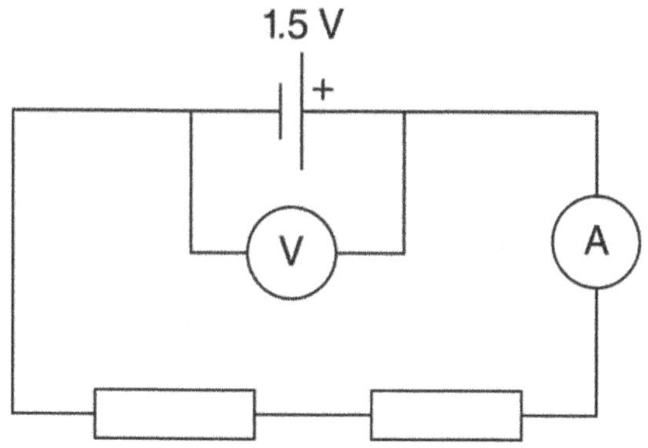

1.5 V

02.1 Which statement about the circuit is correct?

Tick **one** box.

The resistors are connected in parallel. ☐

The current through each resistor has a different value. ☐

The resistors are connected in series. ☐

[1 mark]

02.2 The resistors are identical. Each of the resistors has a resistance of 5.0 Ω

Calculate the total resistance of the two resistors in the circuit in **Figure 2.1**.

Total resistance = _____ Ω

[1 mark]

Question 2 continues on the next page

02.3 The cell in the circuit of **Figure 2.1** supplies a potential difference of 1.5 V

Calculate the size of the electric current from the cell.

Use the following equation.

$$\text{current} = \frac{\text{potential difference}}{\text{resistance}}$$

Current = ... A

[2 marks]

02.4 One of the resistors in **Figure 2.1** is replaced by a resistor with a resistance of 10 Ω

Which **two** statements correctly describe the effect this change has on the circuit?

Tick **two** boxes.

Ammeter reading decreases ☐

Ammeter reading increases ☐

Ammeter reading doesn't change ☐

Voltmeter reading decreases ☐

Voltmeter reading increases ☐

Voltmeter reading doesn't change ☐

[2 marks]

03

03.1 The symbol for a nucleus of one of the isotopes of iodine is:

$$^{127}_{53}\text{I}$$

Give the numbers of protons, neutrons and electrons in an atom of this isotope.

Protons: ....

Neutrons: ....

Electrons: ....

[3 marks]

03.2 Another isotope of iodine is iodine-131.

This isotope undergoes radioactive decay.

Describe what is meant by **radioactive decay**.

....

....

[2 marks]

03.3 Iodine-131 decays by emitting a beta particle.

Explain what is meant by **emitting a beta particle**.

....

....

[2 marks]

Question 3 continues on the next page

03.4 A detector is used to measure the activity of a sample of a radioactive isotope.

The activity of the sample decreases as time passes.

Describe how the activity measurements can be used to determine an accurate value for the half-life of the isotope.

State any other piece of apparatus that may be needed.

....

....

....

....

....

....

....

....

[4 marks]

04 A student is asked to determine the density of a rectangular metal block from a school laboratory materials kit.

She measures the dimensions and the mass of the block.

Her measurements are shown in **Table 4.1**.

Table 4.1

Mass in g	Length in cm	Width in cm	Height in cm
144	5.0	2.0	2.0

04.1 Use the equation below to calculate the volume of the metal block.

volume = length × width × height

Volume = ... cm³

[1 mark]

04.2 Write down the equation which links density, volume and mass.

[1 mark]

04.3 Calculate the density of the metal block.

Density = ... g/cm³

[2 marks]

Question 4 continues on the next page

04.4 The materials kit contains metal blocks made of steel, tin and zinc.

The density of each of these metals is given in **Table 4.2**.

Table 4.2

Metal	steel	tin	zinc
Density in g/cm³	7.850	7.280	7.135

The student decides that her measurements confirm that the block is made of **zinc**.

Suggest why her measurements can **only** confirm that the block is made from **either zinc or tin**.

....

....

....

[1 mark]

05 A student wants to investigate how the resistance of a wire depends on its length.

05.1 Identify the **independent variable**, the **dependent variable** and the **control variable** in this investigation.

Independent variable: ....

Dependent variable: ....

Control variable: ....

[3 marks]

05.2 **Figure 5.1** shows a circuit that can be used to determine the resistance of a length of wire.

The wire under test is connected between crocodile clips X and Y.

Describe how the student could use this circuit in her investigation.

Include any additional apparatus that you think she may need.

Figure 5.1

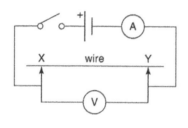

[4 marks]

Question 5 continues on the next page

05.3 The student decides to take repeat measurements for each length of wire.

What type of error does the repeat of measurements help to reduce?

Tick **one** box.

Zero error ☐

Systematic error ☐

Random error ☐

[1 mark]

05.4 The resistance of the student's wire is **directly proportional** to its length.

Sketch a graph on the axes in **Figure 5.2** to show this relationship.

Figure 5.2

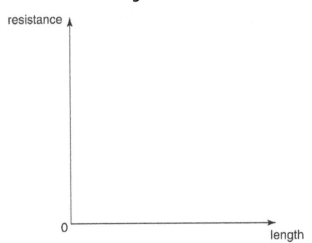

[1 mark]

06   A student was asked to determine the specific heat capacity of a metal block.

06.1   Explain what is meant by **specific heat capacity**.

....

....

[1 mark]

06.2   The student tied a piece of string around the metal block and heated the block to 100°C.

He then lowered the block into a glass beaker containing water at a temperature of 20°C, as shown in **Figure 6.1.**

Figure 6.1

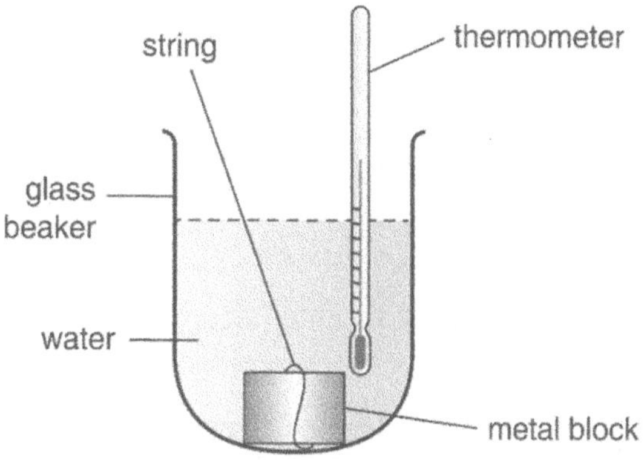

What happened to the block's store of thermal energy when it was placed in the water?

Tick **one** box.

It increased.   ☐

It did not change.   ☐

It decreased.   ☐

[1 mark]

Question 6 continues on the next page

06.3 The student found that the metal block caused the temperature of the water in the beaker to rise by 10°C.

The mass of water in the beaker is 0.10 kg.

The specific heat capacity of water is 4200 J/ kg °C.

Calculate the increase in thermal energy of the water.

Use the following equation.

Change in thermal energy = mass × specific heat capacity × temperature change

Increase in thermal energy of water = ... J

[2 marks]

06.4 When the metal block was put into the water, the block's temperature decreased by 70°C.

The following equation can be used to calculate the specific heat capacity of the block.

$$\text{specific heat capacity} = \frac{\text{loss of thermal energy of block}}{\text{mass} \times \text{temperature decrease}}$$

The mass of the block is 0.10 kg.

The student assumed that all the thermal energy lost by the block was transferred to the water.

Using this assumption, calculate the specific heat capacity of the metal block.

Specific heat capacity = ... J/ kg °C

[2 marks]

06.5 The student's assumption that all the thermal energy lost by the block was transferred to the water may not be correct.

Suggest where else some of the block's thermal energy might have been transferred.

_____

[1 mark]

06.6 Suggest **one** improvement to the experiment to try to ensure that **all** of the block's thermal energy is transferred to the water.

_____

_____

[1 mark]

07

07.1 UK power stations use a range of different fuels to generate electricity.

Which fuel listed below is **not** a fossil fuel?

Tick **one** box.

Coal ☐

Uranium ☐

Natural gas ☐

[1 mark]

07.2 Wind turbines and coal fuelled power stations are both used to generate electricity in the UK.

Compare the use of wind turbines and coal fuelled power stations.

Consider their **reliability** and **environmental effects**.

....

....

....

....

....

....

....

....

....

....

....

....

[6 marks]

08.1 Write down the equation that links gravitational field strength, gravitational potential energy, height and mass.

_____

[1 mark]

08.2 A child rides her bicycle to the top of a small hill and stops.

The height of the hill is 10 m

The mass of the child and her bicycle is 50 kg

Gravitational field strength = 9.8 N/kg

Calculate the increase in the store of gravitational potential energy of the child and her bicycle.

_____

Increase in gravitational potential energy store = _____ J

[2 marks]

08.3 The child now freewheels down the hill on her bicycle.

Her speed is increasing.

What energy transfer is taking place?

Tick **one** box.

Gravitational potential energy to kinetic energy ☐

Kinetic energy to gravitational potential energy ☐

Thermal energy to chemical energy ☐

[1 mark]

08.4 Write down the equation which links kinetic energy, mass and velocity.

_____

[1 mark]

Question 8 continues on the next page

08.5 As the child gets to the bottom of the hill, her speed has reached 6.0 m/s.

Calculate the increase in the store of kinetic energy of the child and her bicycle.

Increase in kinetic energy store = _____ J

[2 marks]

08.6 As the child freewheeled down the hill, some of her energy was dissipated to the surroundings as thermal energy.

This was partly caused by friction in the wheel axles.

Suggest what could be done to reduce this friction.

[1 mark]

09   Coconut oil, used in cooking, is solid at room or fridge temperature.

09.1   A sample of coconut oil from a fridge is heated at a constant rate using an electrical heater.

The graph in **Figure 9.1** shows how the temperature of the oil changes as time passes.

Figure 9.1

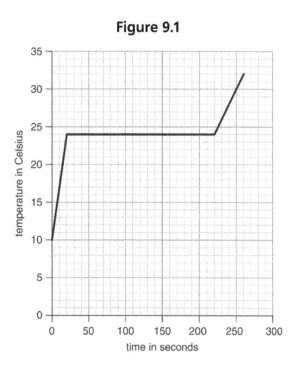

Use **Figure 9.1** to determine the time taken for the sample to undergo the change of state from solid to liquid.

Time taken = ... s

[2 marks]

Question 9 continues on the next page

09.2 Describe three changes to the arrangement **and** the motion of the particles when the coconut oil changes from a solid to a liquid.

_____

_____

_____

_____

[3 marks]

09.3 The power of the heater is 100 W

Write down the equation that links energy transferred with power and time.

_____

[1 mark]

09.4 Calculate the thermal energy transferred to the coconut oil while it is melting.

_____

_____

Energy transferred = _____ J

[2 marks]

09.5 Calculate the specific latent heat of fusion of coconut oil.

The mass of the coconut oil is 0.080 kg

Use the correct equation from the Physics Equation Sheet.

....

....

Specific latent heat of fusion = ... J/kg

[2 marks]

END OF QUESTIONS

Physics Equation Sheet

Equation Number	Word Equation	Symbol Equation
1	(final velocity)^2 − (initial velocity)^2 = 2 × acceleration × distance	$v^2 - u^2 = 2\,a\,s$
2	elastic potential energy = 0.5 × spring constant × (extension)^2	$E_e = \dfrac{1}{2}\,k\,e^2$
3	change in thermal energy = mass × specific heat capacity × temperature change	$\Delta E = m\,c\,\Delta\Theta$
4	period = $\dfrac{1}{\text{frequency}}$	
5	thermal energy for a change of state = mass × specific latent heat	$E = mL$

©HarperCollins*Publishers* 2019

Collins

AQA
GCSE
Combined Science: Trilogy F
SET A – Physics: Paper 6 Foundation Tier
Author: Lynn Pharaoh

Materials   Time allowed: 1 hour 15 minutes

For this paper you must have:

- a ruler
- a calculator
- the Physics Equation Sheet (found at the end of the paper).

Instructions

- Answer all questions in the spaces provided.
- Do all rough work in this book. Cross through any work you do not want to be marked.

Information

- There are 70 marks available on this paper.
- The marks for questions are shown in brackets.
- You are expected to use a calculator where appropriate.
- You are reminded of the need for good English and clear presentation in your answers.
- When answering questions 02.4 and 07.1 you need to make sure that your answer:
  - is clear, logical, sensibly structured
  - fully meets the requirements of the question
  - shows that each separate point or step supports the overall answer.

Advice

- In all calculations, show clearly how you work out your answer.

Name: ....

01

01.1 Give an example of a **contact force**.

....

[1 mark]

01.2 Give an example of a **non-contact force**.

....

[1 mark]

01.3 **Figure 1.1** shows a mass supported by a piece of string wrapped around an axle.

Figure 1.1

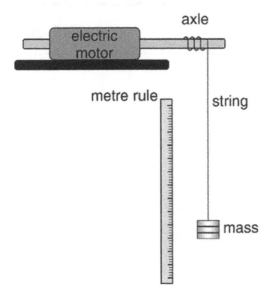

Name the **two** forces acting on the mass while it is held stationary.

1. ....

2. ....

[2 marks]

01.4 When the motor is switched on, the mass is winched upwards at a steady speed.

The force needed to lift the mass is 4.0 N

Calculate the work done by the motor in raising the mass a distance of 0.25 m

Use the following equation:

work done = force × distance

Work done = ... N m

[2 marks]

02.1 Complete the following sentences about magnets.

Use the correct words from the box.

an attractive force	a repulsive force	no force

The north pole of one magnet exerts .... on the south pole of a second magnet.

The north pole of a magnet exerts .... on a piece of magnetic material such as iron.

The north pole of one magnet exerts .... on the north pole of a second magnet.

The south pole of one magnet exerts .... on the south pole of a second magnet.

[4 marks]

02.2 Describe the differences between a **permanent magnet** and an **induced magnet**.

....

....

....

....

....

[3 marks]

02.3 The region around a magnet is called a **magnetic field**.

Figure 2.1 shows two magnetic field lines in the space around a bar magnet.

Add an arrow to **both** of the field lines to show the direction of the magnetic field.

Figure 2.1

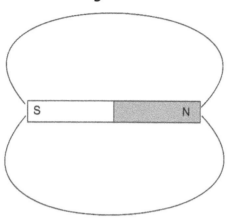

[2 marks]

Question 2 continues on the next page

02.4 Write a set of instructions for plotting a magnetic field line around a bar magnet using a compass.

You may include a diagram as part of your answer.

....

....

....

....

....

....

....

[4 marks]

03

03.1 Which **two** statements correctly represent Newton's first law of motion?

Tick **two** boxes.

The resultant force on a stationary object is zero. ☐

Acceleration is proportional to resultant force. ☐

When two objects exert forces on each other, the forces are equal and opposite. ☐

The resultant force on an object moving at a steady speed is zero. ☐

[2 marks]

03.2 **Figure 3.1** shows a van travelling along a straight road.

The arrows represent the forces acting on the van.

Figure 3.1

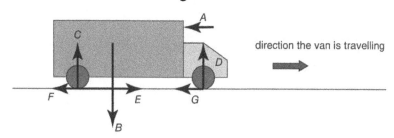

Which arrow in **Figure 3.1** represents the driving force from the van's engine?

Tick **one** box.

A	B	C	D	E	F	G

[1 mark]

Question 3 continues on the next page

03.3 Which **two** forces shown in **Figure 3.1** represent friction between the tyres and the road?

Tick **two** boxes.

A	B	C	D	E	F	G

[2 marks]

03.4 Which force in **Figure 3.1** represents the weight of the van?

Tick **one** box.

A	B	C	D	E	F	G

[1 mark]

03.5 Which force in **Figure 3.1** represents air resistance acting on the van?

Tick **one** box.

A	B	C	D	E	F	G

[1 mark]

03.6 The van in **Figure 3.1** is travelling at a velocity of 10 m/s

The van now accelerates to a velocity of 14 m/s

It takes 2.5 s to reach a velocity of 14 m/s

Use the following equation to calculate the van's acceleration.

$$acceleration = \frac{change\ in\ velocity}{time}$$

Give the correct unit with your answer.

_____

_____

Acceleration = _____

Unit: _____

[3 marks]

03.7 The mass of the van is 4000 kg

Calculate the resultant force acting on the van while it is accelerating.

Use the following equation.

resultant force = mass × acceleration

Resultant force = _____ N

[2 marks]

04   **Figure 4.1** shows a plan view of a ripple tank used to investigate the behaviour of waves.

Figure 4.1

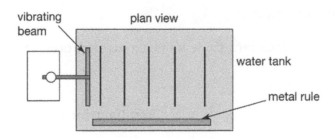

04.1 The vibrating beam in the ripple tank produces waves which travel across the tank.

The frequency of the vibrating beam can be changed.

Explain the word **frequency** in this case.

....

....

[1 mark]

04.2 The vibrating beam makes 20 waves in 4 s

What is the frequency of the waves?

Tick **one** box.

20 Hz   ☐

5.0 Hz   ☐

80 Hz   ☐

[1 mark]

04.3 The parallel lines on the ripple tank in **Figure 4.1** represent lines of wave crests.

Give the name of the distance from one line of crests to the next line of crests.

....

[1 mark]

04.4 **Figure 4.2** shows a side view of the ripple tank.

The waves on the water are travelling from left to right.

Figure 4.2

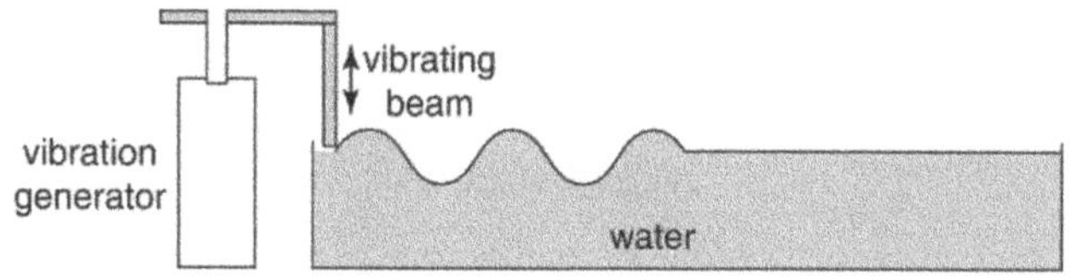

What type of wave is shown on the water in **Figure 4.2**?

Tick **one** box.

Transverse ☐

Longitudinal ☐

[1 mark]

04.5 A teacher wants to use the ripple tank in **Figure 4.2** to demonstrate that it is the wave and not the water that travels across the tank.

Describe how this could be done.

....

....

....

[2 marks]

Question 4 continues on the next page

04.6 Write down the equation that links wave speed, frequency and wavelength.

_____

[1 mark]

04.7 The frequency of the waves on the ripple tank is changed to 3.0 Hz

The wavelength of the waves is measured at 4.0 cm

Calculate the speed of these ripple tank waves.

_____

_____

Wave speed = _____ cm/s

[2 marks]

04.8 A student investigates how the speed of a wave on water varies with the depth of the water.

Identify the **independent variable** and the **dependent variable**.

Independent variable: _____

Dependent variable: _____

[2 marks]

04.9 **Figure 4.3** is a sketch graph of the student's results.

Figure 4.3

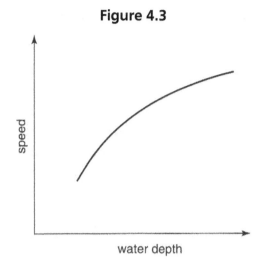

Give **two** conclusions from the graph.

1. ....

....

2. ....

....

[2 marks]

05

05.1 Name **one** quantity that has both magnitude and direction.

....

[1 mark]

05.2 **Figure 5.1** represents the motion of a car on a straight road.

Figure 5.1

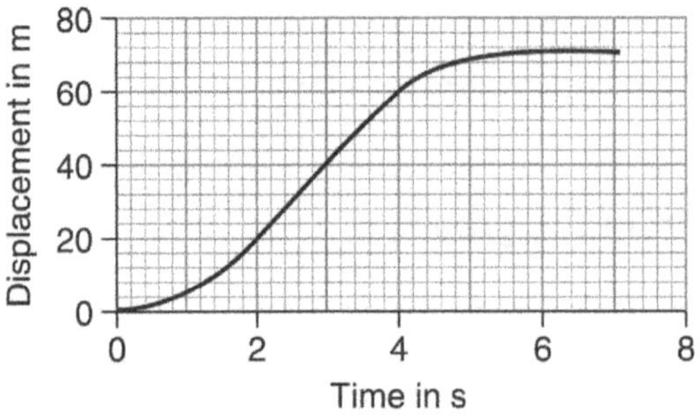

Use **Figure 5.1** to give **two** conclusions about the car's journey.

1. ....

....

2. ....

....

[2 marks]

05.3 Use **Figure 5.1** to determine the displacement of the car at 4 s.

Displacement = ... m

[1 mark]

05.4 Write down the equation that links distance travelled, speed and time.

....

05.5 Calculate the average speed of the car during the first 4 s of the car's motion.

Use data from **Figure 5.1**.

....

....

Average speed = ... m/s

[2 marks]

06 A student uses the apparatus in **Figure 6.1** to investigate the rate of emission of infrared radiation from different surfaces.

Figure 6.1

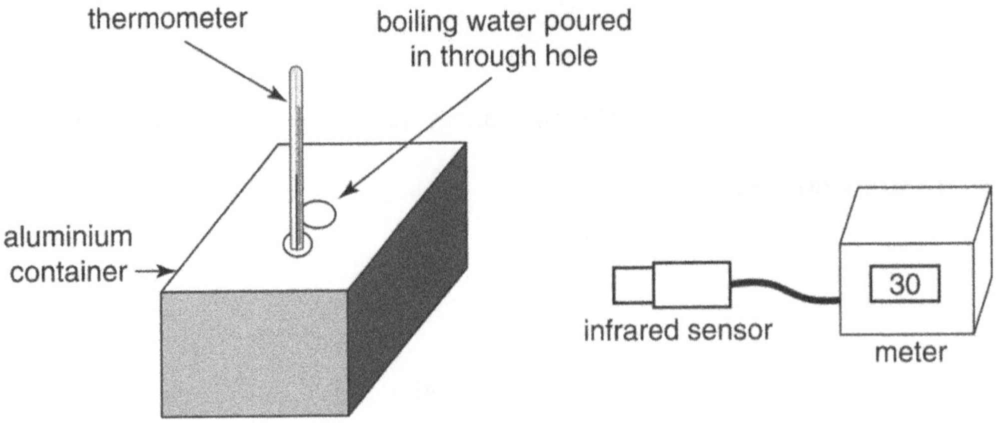

The student pours boiling water into the aluminium container. This raises the temperature of the container.

The intensity of the infrared radiation from the container's surface is measured by the infrared sensor and displayed on the meter.

The four vertical faces of the container have a different type of surface:

- polished aluminium

- dull aluminium

- shiny black

- dull black.

The student points the infrared sensor at each of the four surfaces in turn and records the meter readings.

06.1 The student wants to carry out the investigation as a fair test.

He must take the readings quickly so that the thermometer reading remains the same for all four measurements.

Explain why it is important that the thermometer reading is the same for all four measurements.

....

....

....

[1 mark]

06.2 When he takes the infrared readings, the student positions the sensor 10 cm from each surface.

Explain why the sensor must be at the same distance from each surface when the infrared readings are taken.

....

....

....

[1 mark]

06.3 The student's readings are displayed on the chart in **Figure 6.2**.

Figure 6.2

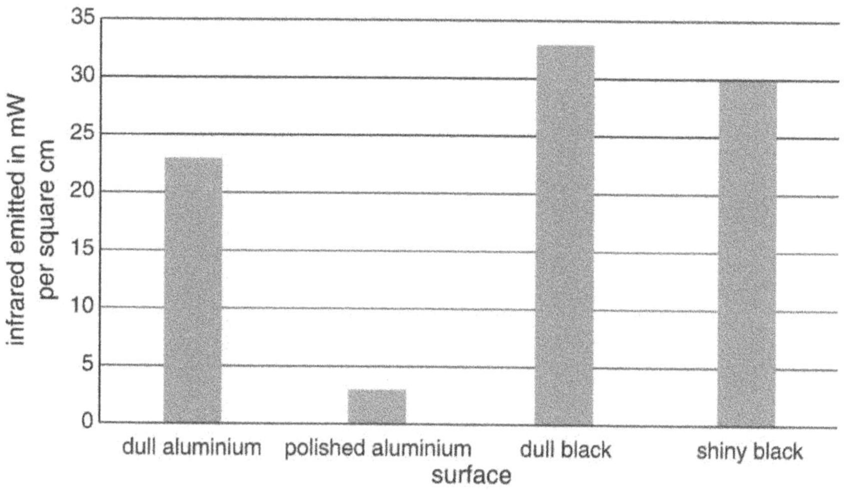

Give **two** conclusions based on **Figure 6.2**.

1. ....

....

2. ....

....

[2 marks]

Question 6 continues on the next page

06.4 The student found it difficult to take the readings from the four surfaces quickly.

The reading on the thermometer dropped each time.

Suggest an improvement to the experiment so that there is no need to take all four readings quickly.

....

....

....

[1 mark]

07 A student is asked to use the apparatus in **Figure 7.1** to obtain a series of measurements of extension of a spring.

She has a range of standard weights to attach to the spring.

Figure 7.1

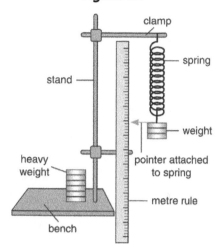

07.1 Write a set of instructions that the student could follow to obtain the measurements **as accurately as possible**.

....

....

....

....

....

....

....

....

....

....

....

....

[6 marks]

Question 7 continues on the next page

07.2 The student repeats the experiment for two more springs.

Data for the three springs, **A**, **B** and **C**, are displayed on the graph in **Figure 7.2**.

Figure 7.2

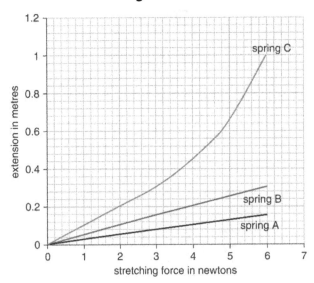

Which **one** of the springs has been stretched beyond its limit of proportionality?

Tick **one** box.

A ☐

B ☐

C ☐

[1 mark]

07.3 Which **one** of the springs is the easiest to stretch?

Tick **one** box.

A ☐

B ☐

C ☐

[1 mark]

07.4 Which **one** of the springs has the greatest spring constant?

Use the data shown in **Figure 7.2**.

Tick **one** box.

A ☐

B ☐

C ☐

[1 mark]

07.5 Which **one** of the springs requires a force of 4.0 N to extend it by 0.20 m?

Use the data shown in **Figure 7.2**.

Tick **one** box.

A ☐

B ☐

C ☐

[1 mark]

07.6 Write down the equation that links force with spring constant and extension of a spring.

_____

[1 mark]

Question 7 continues on the next page

07.7 The unstretched length of a fourth spring, **D**, is 0.085 m

A force of 8.0 N stretches the spring. The new length of the spring is 0.335 m

Calculate the spring constant of spring **D**.

Spring constant = ... N/m

[3 marks]

END OF QUESTIONS

BLANK PAGE

Physics Equation Sheet

Equation Number	Word Equation	Symbol Equation
1	(final velocity)^2 – (initial velocity)^2 = 2 × acceleration × distance	$v^2 - u^2 = 2\,a\,s$
2	elastic potential energy = 0.5 × spring constant × (extension)^2	$E_e = \dfrac{1}{2}\,k\,e^2$
3	change in thermal energy = mass × specific heat capacity × temperature change	$\Delta E = m\,c\,\Delta\Theta$
4	period = $\dfrac{1}{\text{frequency}}$	
5	thermal energy for a change of state = mass × specific latent heat	$E = mL$

Collins

AQA
GCSE
Combined Science: Trilogy   F

SET B – Biology: Paper 1 Foundation Tier

Author: Kath Skillern

Materials

Time allowed: 1 hour 15 minutes

For this paper you must have:

- a ruler
- a calculator.

Instructions

- Answer **all** questions in the spaces provided.
- Do all rough work in this book. Cross through any work you do not want to be marked.

Information

- There are 70 marks available on this paper.
- The marks for questions are shown in brackets.
- You are expected to use a calculator where appropriate.
- You are reminded of the need for good English and clear presentation in your answers.
- When answering questions 06.3 and 07.2 you need to make sure that your answer:
  – is clear, logical, sensibly structured
  – fully meets the requirements of the question
  – shows that each separate point or step supports the overall answer.

Advice

- In all calculations, show clearly how you work out your answer.

Name:

---

01 Pathogens cause diseases in plants and animals.

Plants and animals are able to defend themselves against attack.

01.1 Name **one** of the first physical barriers a pathogen encounters when trying to attack a human.

....

[1 mark]

01.2 White blood cells help to defend the human body against pathogens.

How do white blood cells help to defend the body?

Tick **one** box.

Alcohol production ☐

Antibiotic production ☐

Antibody production ☐

Antigen production ☐

[1 mark]

01.3 Which of the diagrams below represents a white blood cell?

The diagrams are **not** to scale.

Tick **one** box.

☐   ☐   ☐   **[1 mark]**

01.4 Describe how antibiotics can be used to treat diseases.

....

....

....

[2 marks]

01.5 Describe how antibiotics are different from painkillers.

....

....

....

[2 marks]

Question 1 continues on the next page

Jon has a greenhouse and grows a variety of plants.

He notices that some of his plants appear unhealthy.

01.6 What type of organism causes tobacco mosaic disease in plants?

_____

[1 mark]

01.7 Describe the appearance of the leaves of a plant suffering from this disease.

_____

_____

[1 mark]

01.8 Which of these diseases is caused by a fungus?

Tick **one** box.

Aphids   ☐

Black spot   ☐

Gonorrhoea   ☐

Salmonella   ☐

[1 mark]

02   The digestive system is a collection of organs that work together to digest and absorb our food.

02.1   What is the name given to biological molecules that break down our food?

Tick **one** box.

Catalysts ☐

Enzymes ☐

Proteins ☐

Substrate ☐

[1 mark]

02.2   Jon ate a sausage sandwich.

Complete the following sentences:

* Proteases break down proteins to _____ .

* Glycerol and fatty acids are produced when lipases break down

   _____ .

[2 marks]

Question 2 continues on the next page

02.3 Amylase is a carbohydrase which breaks down starch to maltose and glucose.

Jon wanted to investigate the effect of pH on the rate of reaction of amylase.

This is the method used.

1. Gather three solutions:

    • amylase

    • starch solution

    • pH buffer solution.

2. Set up a spotting tile with rows of iodine drops and prepare the stopwatch.

3. Mix the three solutions in a test tube in a particular order and start the stopwatch.

Jon added the solutions to the test tube in this order:

1. amylase solution

2. buffer solution

3. starch solution.

He then started the stopwatch.

Explain why it is important that Jon mixed the solutions in this order.

_____

_____

[1 mark]

                    ©HarperCollins*Publishers* 2019

02.4 Every 10 seconds, Jon used a pipette to place a drop of the mix onto the next iodine drop in the spotting tile.

He repeated this until the iodine remained orange after the mix was added.

He also set up a colour control with iodine and water.

Explain why a control might help.

_____

_____

_____

[2 marks]

02.5 **Table 2.1** shows some results from the investigation.

Table 2.1

pH of solution	5	6	7	8	9
Times for colour change to occur (seconds)					
Test 1	160	75	50	85	85
Test 2	150	70	40	80	95
Test 3	150	75	40	75	90
Mean	153	73	43		90

Calculate the mean time for colour change to occur for the pH 8 solution.

Mean = _____

Units = _____

[3 marks]

Question 2 continues on the next page

02.6 Which is the optimum pH for amylase to work?

Tick **one** box.

pH 5 ☐

pH 6 ☐

pH 7 ☐

pH 8 ☐

pH 9 ☐

[1 mark]

03 Plant and animal cells have different characteristics.

03.1 Draw **one** line from each cell characteristic to the correct type of cell.

Cell characteristic

Plant cell		Animal cell
	Plasma membrane only, no cell wall	
	Carbohydrate stored as glycogen	
	Chloroplasts	
	Large vacuole	

[3 marks]

Question 3 continues on the next page

03.2 When using a microscope, live cells can be mounted in a drop of water on a microscope slide.

They are then covered using a transparent coverslip.

Which of the following is a reason for using a coverslip?

Tick **one** box.

To kill the specimen	☐
To keep the specimen flat	☐
To preserve the specimen	☐
To trap air in the specimen	☐

[1 mark]

03.3 Which stain is used to add colour and contrast to plant cells to look at them under the microscope?

Tick **one** box.

Hydrogen peroxide	☐
Iodine solution	☐
Methylene blue	☐
Potassium dichromate	☐

[1 mark]

03.4 Figure 3.1 shows a low-power micrograph of a plant root. The root is approximately 2mm in diameter just below the meristem.

Figure 3.1

Draw a diagram of the plant root.

Label the meristem on your diagram.

Draw an appropriate scale bar on your diagram.

[4 marks]

Turn over >

04 An estimated 42% of cancer cases each year in the UK are linked to lifestyle choices.

Look at **Figure 4.1**.

Figure 4.1

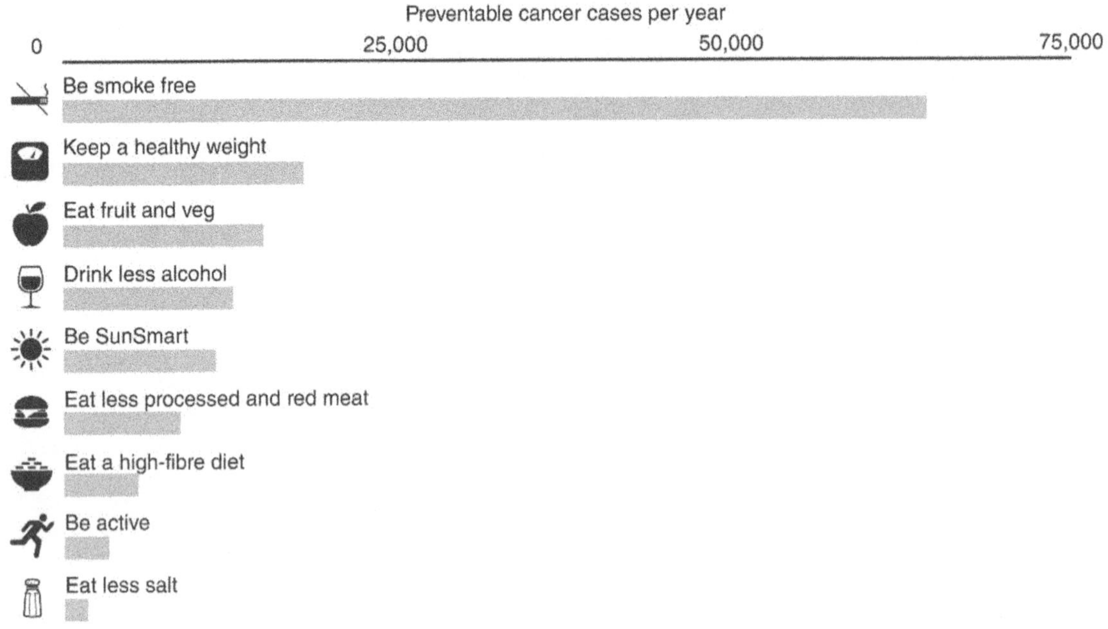

Preventable cancer cases per year

04.1 Compare the numbers of preventable cancers related to **being active** with those related to **drinking less alcohol**.

Number of cancers related to being active: ....

Number of cancers related to drinking less alcohol: ....

Comparison: ....

....

[2 marks]

04.2 Use the data in **Figure 4.1** to describe a healthy diet to reduce the risk of developing cancer.

....

....

[2 marks]

04.3 Tobacco is by far the most common cause of cancer in the UK.

What type of cancer is commonly linked with tobacco smoking?

....

[1 mark]

04.4 Describe the difference between a benign tumour and a malignant tumour.

Benign tumour:

....

[1 mark]

Malignant tumour:

....

....

[2 marks]

Turn over >

05 A vaccination introduces a small quantity of dead pathogen into the body to protect us from disease.

A new vaccination has been developed against the pathogen Lumpius.

The Lumpius vaccine is being tested by a pharmaceutical company, which has recruited 10 000 volunteers.

Figure 5.1 shows the body's response to the vaccination and later to infection by Lumpius.

Figure 5.1

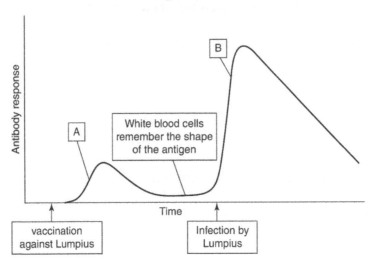

05.1 Explain why antibodies are being produced at A.

....

....

....

[1 mark]

05.2 Why is the antibody response much bigger at B compared with A?

....

....

....

[2 marks]

05.3 Explain why the pharmaceutical company thinks that the vaccine is effective.

....

....

....

[2 marks]

05.4 Describe the development process for a new vaccination, such as Lumpius.

....

....

....

....

[3 marks]

Turn over >

06   Jane has set up equipment to investigate the rate of photosynthesis in an aquatic plant.

She uses a lamp as a light source.

Figure 6.1

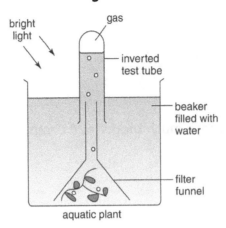

06.1 Describe how Jane can vary the light intensity to be an independent variable.

....

....

[2 marks]

06.2 Describe how Jane can record the production rate of oxygen.

....

....

[1 mark]

06.3 Explain how Jane should carry out her investigation.

[6 marks]

06.4 Jane wants a pond in her garden to keep fish.

Explain why she should dig her pond in a sunny part of the garden.

[2 marks]

07   Figure 7.1 shows a plant cell under a microscope.

Figure 7.1

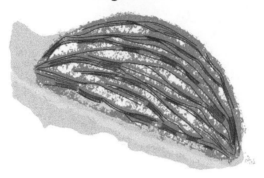

07.1 What is the name of this structure?

Tick **one** box.

Chloroplast ☐

Cytoplasm ☐

Nucleus ☐

Vacuole ☐

[1 mark]

07.2 During photosynthesis, plants harness the Sun's energy and make food.

Describe photosynthesis, the factors that affect it and how plants use the products.

_____

_____

_____

_____

_____

_____

_____

_____

[6 marks]

08   **Figure 8.1** shows two different types of fox.

Fennec foxes live in hot desert areas. Arctic foxes live in cold regions.

Figure 8.1

Fennec fox   Arctic fox

Their ears are not regular shapes.

To measure the surface areas of the ears, Sue:
- takes measurements of the left ear of a fox

- draws the shape of the ear onto graph paper

- uses the graph paper to help her find the surface area of the ear.

Figure 8.2 shows the measurements of the left ear of an Arctic fox drawn on graph paper.
Each large square is 1 cm × 1 cm

The diagram is **not** to scale.

Figure 8.2

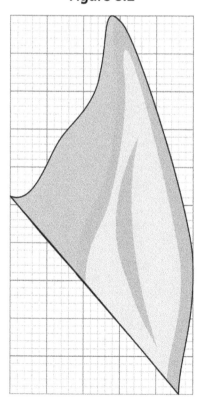

Question 8 continues on the next page

08.1 What is the surface area of one side of the Arctic fox's ear?

Surface area ....

Units ....

[2 marks]

08.2 The surface area of one side of the Fennec fox's ear is 228 cm².

Calculate how much bigger the Fennec fox's ear is, when compared with the Arctic fox's ear.

Write this as a percentage.

Give your answer using an appropriate number of significant figures.

Size of Fennec fox's ear = 228 cm²

Size of Arctic fox's ear = ... (your answer to **08.1** from above)

....

....

....

....

The Fennec fox's ear is bigger by: .... %

[3 marks]

08.3 Suggest a reason why Fennec foxes may have **larger** ears than Arctic foxes.

....

....

....

....

[2 marks]

END OF QUESTIONS

Collins

AQA
GCSE
Combined Science: Trilogy   F
SET B – Biology: Paper 2 Foundation Tier
Author: Kath Skillern

Materials

Time allowed: 1 hour 15 minutes

> **For this paper you must have:**
> - a ruler
> - a calculator.

Instructions

- Answer **all** questions in the spaces provided.
- Do all rough work in this book. Cross through any work you do not want to be marked.

Information

- There are 70 marks available on this paper.
- The marks for questions are shown in brackets.
- You are expected to use a calculator where appropriate.
- You are reminded of the need for good English and clear presentation in your answers.

Advice

- In all calculations, show clearly how you work out your answer.

Name: ....

01 An ecosystem is the interaction of a community of living organisms with the non-living parts of their environment.

01.1 How is the **non-living** part of the environment described?

Tick **one** box.

Abiotic ☐

Biotic ☐

Dead ☐

Habitat ☐

[1 mark]

01.2 Name **two** resources that **plants** compete for.

1. ....

2. ....

[2 marks]

01.3 Name **two** resources that **animals** compete for.

1. ....

2. ....

[2 marks]

01.4 Within a community each species depends on other species to help it survive.

If one species is removed it can affect the whole community.

How is this described?

Tick **one** box.

Interaction ☐

Interdependence ☐

Ecosystem ☐

Environment ☐

[1 mark]

01.5 Explain the term 'a **stable community**'.

....

....

....

[2 marks]

01.6 Which **two** materials do microorganisms cycle through an ecosystem?

Tick **two** boxes.

Carbon dioxide ☐

Compost ☐

Mineral ions ☐

Oxygen ☐

Water ☐

[2 marks]

Turn over >

02 The human body reacts to changes by coordinating a **nervous** response or a **hormonal** response.

02.1 Draw a line from each response description to **either** the nervous system **or** the hormonal system.

System	Response description	System

Fast acting

Slow acting

Acts for short time

Acts for long time

Nervous system

Hormonal system

Chemical

Electrical

Acts in a specific area

Acts more generally

[4 marks]

02.2 The control of blood glucose concentration is one example of **homeostasis**.

Name **one** other example of homeostasis in the body.

....

[1 mark]

02.3 Automatic control systems may involve nervous responses or chemical responses.

All control systems include receptors, coordination centres and effectors.

Give **one** location in the body of **receptor cells**.

....

[1 mark]

02.4 Give **one** example of a **coordination centre**.

....

[1 mark]

02.5 Give **one** example of an **effector.**

....

[1 mark]

Question 2 continues on the next page

02.6 In a scientific study, called **Scientific Study A**, reaction times were investigated after four volunteers had drunk alcohol.

A small can of beer contains about one unit of alcohol.

The results are shown in **Table 2.1**.

Table 2.1

Volunteer		Reaction time in milliseconds (ms)				
	Units of alcohol	0.5	1.5	3.0	4.5	6.0
A		34	45	59	71	85
B		35	47	62	75	87
C		32	46	64	72	83
D		30	42	59	70	81
Mean		33	45	61	72	

Calculate the mean reaction time of the volunteers after 6.0 units of alcohol.

....

....

Mean reaction time after 6.0 units of alcohol = ...

[3 marks]

02.7 What do these results suggest about the effect of drinking alcohol on reaction times?

....

....

[1 mark]

03 Type 2 diabetes is a serious condition.

In Type 2 diabetes the body's cells no longer respond as effectively to control glucose concentration in the blood.

Look at **Table 3.1**.

Table 3.1

Year	Percentage (%) of the population who have Type 2 diabetes	Mean body mass in kg
1990	4.9	72.5
1991	5.0	73.0
1992	5.4	73.7
1993	4.7	74.0
1994	5.3	74.6
1995	5.5	75.0
1996	5.4	74.8
1997	6.2	75.3
1998	6.5	76.0
1999	6.9	76.6
2000	7.3	77.2

Question 3 continues on the next page

03.1 Use the data in **Table 3.1** to plot a graph to show the effect of body mass on the percentage of the population who have Type 2 diabetes.

You do not need to use the Year column in **Table 3.1**.

Make sure to:

- choose an appropriate scale
- label both axes
- plot all points to show the pattern of results.

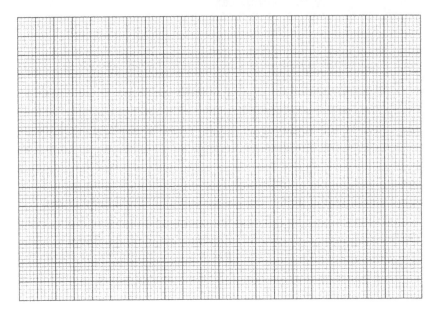

[4 marks]

03.2 Describe the relationship between the mean body mass of the population and the percentage of people who have Type 2 diabetes.

....

....

[1 mark]

03.3 Hormones control reproduction:

- Follicle stimulating hormone (FSH) causes maturation of an egg in the ovary.
- Oestrogen and progesterone are involved in maintaining the uterus lining.

Use this information to explain how **one hormonal** method of contraception works.

....

....

....

[2 marks]

Turn over >

04   Evolutionary trees are used by scientists to show how organisms are related.

Figure 4.1 shows an evolutionary tree.

The numbers on the branches of the evolutionary tree are the number of 'million years ago'.

Figure 4.1

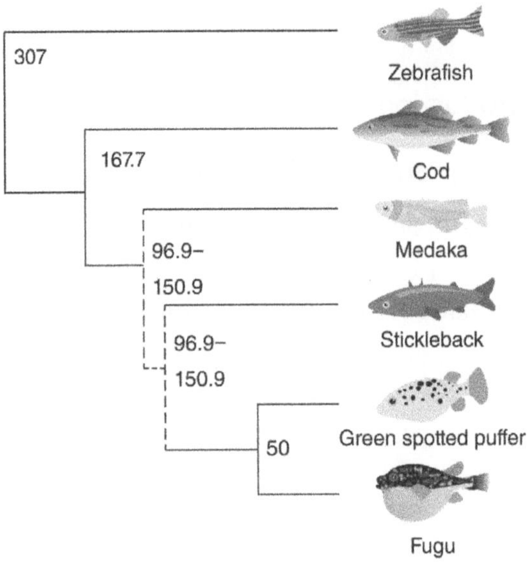

04.1 Which fish is the most **distantly** related to the others?

Tick **one** box.

Cod   ☐

Fugu   ☐

Green spotted puffer   ☐

Medaka   ☐

Stickleback   ☐

Zebrafish   ☐

[1 mark]

04.2 Which **two** fishes are most **closely** related?

Tick **two** boxes.

Cod ☐

Fugu ☐

Green spotted puffer ☐

Medaka ☐

Stickleback ☐

Zebrafish ☐

[1 mark]

04.3 How long ago did the cod split from medaka and stickleback?

....

[1 mark]

04.4 Suggest why there is only a **dotted** line between medaka and stickleback.

....

....

[1 mark]

04.5 Suggest **one** reason why the green spotted puffer and fugu are described as different species.

....

....

[2 marks]

04.6 Name **one** type of evidence that helps scientists construct evolutionary trees.

....

[1 mark]

Turn over >

05   Sexual reproduction involves the joining of male and female gametes.

05.1 What is the male gamete in **plants**?

....

[1 mark]

05.2 Asexual reproduction involves only one parent and no joining of gametes.

This creates genetically identical offspring.

What is the type of cell division that creates genetically identical offspring?

....

[1 mark]

05.3 Describe the process of the formation of gametes in reproductive organs.

....

....

....

[2 marks]

05.4 Some of the characteristics of living things are controlled by a single gene, such as fur colour in mice.

Figure 5.1 shows the alleles for fur colour in three mice.

Figure 5.1

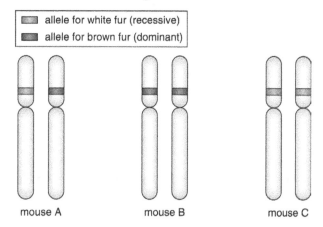

How are the alleles of Mouse A described?

Tick **one** box.

Dominant ☐

Heterozygous ☐

Homozygous ☐

Phenotype ☐

[1 mark]

Question 5 continues on the next page

05.5 Which mouse or mice have brown fur?

Tick **one** box.

Mouse B only ☐

Mice A and B ☐

Mouse A only ☐

Mice A and C ☐

[1 mark]

05.6 If Mouse B and Mouse C were to breed, what colour fur would their offspring have?

....

[1 mark]

05.7 Explain your answer to question 05.6.

....

....

....

....

....

[3 marks]

05.8 Like humans, mice are mammals. Describe the sex chromosomes of a male mouse.

....

[1 mark]

05.9 A gardener has been breeding roses in her garden.

She selects the roses with the biggest blossoms and most fragrant flowers to breed together, and pollinates them herself.

How is the gardener's method of breeding described?

....

[1 mark]

05.10 A farmer's cabbages suffer from white fly.

The farmer asks a local plant laboratory to create him a resistant breed of cabbage.

How is the farmer's method of breeding described?

....

[1 mark]

05.11 Compare the advantages and disadvantages of the gardener's and the farmer's approaches to improving their plants.

....

....

....

....

[2 marks]

Turn over >

06   **Figure 6.1** shows five closely related species of fish, with their diets and habitats.

Figure 6.1

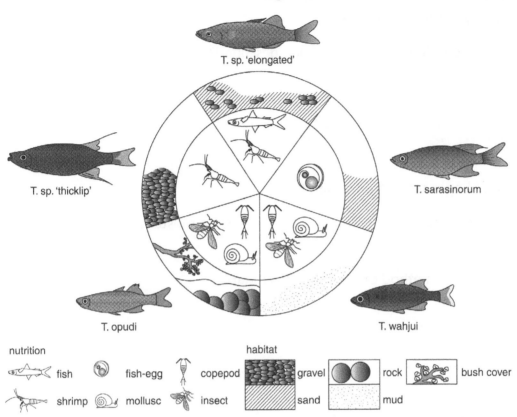

06.1   The copepods in this community are primary consumers.

Suggest what their diet may consist of.

_____

[1 mark]

06.2 In one year, there was a huge increase in the numbers of *T. sarasinorum*.

How would this affect the numbers of 'thicklip'?

Explain your answer.

....

....

....

....

[3 marks]

06.3 Explain why *T. opudi* and *T. wahjui* are **not** competitors, even though they have similar diets.

....

....

....

[2 marks]

06.4 Describe how a new weed disease may cause *T. opudi* to become extinct.

....

....

....

[2 marks]

06.5 Name a source of pollution that could affect the fish.

....

[1 mark]

Turn over >

07.1 Explain the difference between **population size** and **population density**.

....

....

....

....

[2 marks]

07.2 Mr Green needs to assess the population of plantain on a 10 m wide path in a national park.

Figure 7.1 shows broadleaf plantain, which is a tough plant often found on footpaths.

Figure 7.1

Mr Green has a 25 cm² wire quadrat and a measuring tape.

He places the tape across the path, including the dense verges either side of the path.

What is the name of this line?

....

[1 mark]

07.3 Mr Green places the quadrat at the end of the line, in the verge.

He counts the number of whole plants in the quadrat and records the number.

Explain how Mr Green should decide where to place the **next** quadrat along the line.

....

....

....

....

[2 marks]

07.4 Mr Green samples along the line, until he reaches the other end.

The whole path is 500 m long.

Describe the steps Mr Green should follow so that he has statistical evidence for the distribution of plantain **along the length of the path**.

....

....

....

....

[3 marks]

Question 7 continues on the next page

07.5 Explain why there are likely to be more plantains in the **middle** of the path than at the edges.

....

....

[2 marks]

END OF QUESTIONS

Collins

AQA

GCSE

Combined Science: Trilogy F

SET B – Chemistry: Paper 3 Foundation Tier

Author: Paul Lewis

Materials   Time allowed: 1 hour 15 minutes

For this paper you must have:

- a ruler
- a calculator
- the Periodic Table (found at the end of the paper).

Instructions

- Answer all questions in the spaces provided.
- Do all rough work in this book. Cross through any work you do not want to be marked.

Information

- There are 70 marks available on this paper.
- The marks for questions are shown in brackets.
- You are expected to use a calculator where appropriate.
- You are reminded of the need for good English and clear presentation in your answers.
- When answering questions 04.3 and 07.2 you need to make sure that your answer:
  - is clear, logical, sensibly structured
  - fully meets the requirements of the question
  - shows that each separate point or step supports the overall answer.

Advice

- In all calculations, show clearly how you work out your answer.

Name: ....

01

01.1 Which statement about the structure of the atom is **correct**?

Tick **one** box.

The nucleus contains both protons and electrons. ☐

The nucleus contains just protons. ☐

The nucleus contains both protons and neutrons. ☐

The nucleus contains both electrons and neutrons. ☐

[1 mark]

01.2 Draw **one** line from each word to its definition.

Word

element

compound

mixture

Definition

where two or more substances are together but can be separated

a substance that is made from only one type of atom

a substance that contains only neutrons and protons

where two or more substances have chemically combined

[1 mark]

01.3 Which of these atoms are in the same group of the Periodic Table?

Tick **two** boxes.

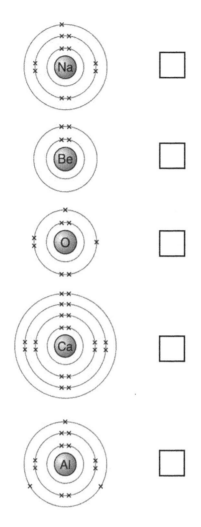

[1 mark]

Question 1 continues on the next page

01.4 Which type of bonding is represented in **Figure 1.1**?

Figure 1.1

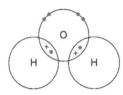

Tick **one** box.

Simple molecular ☐

Giant metallic ☐

Giant covalent ☐

Giant ionic ☐

[1 mark]

01.5 Which of these are properties of most **non-metals**?

Tick **two** boxes.

Sonorous ☐

High melting point ☐

Dull appearance ☐

Dense ☐

Good thermal conductor ☐

Low boiling point ☐

[2 marks]

02.1 **Figure 2.1** shows the location of some of the elements in the Periodic Table.

The letters are **not** the symbols for the elements in that location.

Figure 2.1

A																	Z
											B				X		
	V							D									
												C					
															Y		

Write letters from **Figure 2.1** to identify the following.

A noble gas can be found at letter ....

A Group 5 element can be found at letter ....

An element with 17 electrons can be found at letter ....

An element with only 10 protons can be found at letter ....

[4 marks]

02.2 Group 1 metals all react with water.

State the name of the **gas** given off when this happens.

Describe the laboratory test for this gas.

Name of gas: ....

Test: ....

....

[2 marks]

Question 2 continues on the next page

02.3 The electronic structure of lithium is (2, 1)

When lithium reacts, it forms an ion.

Draw a diagram to show the electronic structure of a lithium ion.

Show the charge on the ion.

[2 marks]

02.4 When lithium reacts with water the following observations can be made:

- Lithium floats on the water

- Lithium moves across the water

- Lithium fizzes

- A gas is given off.

State **three differences** between the reaction of **potassium and water** when compared to the reaction of lithium and water.

1. ....

....

2. ....

....

3. ....

....

[3 marks]

02.5 Explain why the elements in Group 1 get more reactive further down the group, moving from lithium to francium.

....

....

....

....

....

....

....

....

[3 marks]

Turn over >

03 Sodium nitrate ($NaNO_3$), a salt, can be made by a neutralisation reaction.

03.1 At the end of this neutralisation reaction, which of the following is most likely to be the pH of the solution?

Tick **one** box.

3 ☐

5 ☐

7 ☐

9 ☐

[1 mark]

03.2 How many atoms are shown in the empirical formula for sodium nitrate?

Tick **one** box.

3 ☐

4 ☐

5 ☐

6 ☐

[1 mark]

03.3 Calculate the **relative formula mass** of sodium nitrate.

Relative atomic masses: nitrogen = 14; sodium = 23; oxygen = 16

....

....

....

Relative formula mass (M_r) = ...

[2 marks]

03.4 During the neutralisation reaction, sodium hydroxide is reacted with an acid to make sodium nitrate and water.

What is the name of the **acid** used in the reaction?

....

[1 mark]

03.5 Write a **word equation** for the reaction.

.... **+** .... → .... **+** ....

[2 marks]

03.6 Complete the **equation** that represents this reaction.

H^+ **+** .... → H_2O

[1 mark]

04 An atom of hydrogen can be represented by the symbol:

$$^1_1H$$

04.1 How many protons, neutrons and electrons are found in a hydrogen atom?

number of protons: ....

number of electrons: ....

number of neutrons: ....

[3 marks]

04.2 Complete the three missing entries in **Table 4.1**.

Table 4.1

Particle	Relative mass	Charge
neutron		
electron		−1
Proton	1	+1

[2 marks]

04.3 Chlorine is found as isotopes.

Table 4.2 gives two types of chlorine and their relative abundances.

Table 4.2

Isotope	Relative abundance (%)
chlorine-35	75
chlorine-37	25

Describe the structure of the nucleus for both chlorine-35 and chlorine-37.

Explain why they are called **isotopes** of each other.

Use the information above to calculate the relative atomic mass of chlorine.

Give your answer to 3 significant figures.

[6 marks]

05.1 Hydrogen and fluorine can react to form hydrogen fluoride.

The outer shell of each atom is shown in **Figure 5.1**.

Figure 5.1

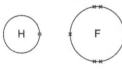

Draw a **dot and cross** diagram for a molecule of hydrogen fluoride.

[2 marks]

05.2 Explain why simple molecules, such as hydrogen and carbon dioxide, are often found as gases at room temperature.

....

....

....

....

[2 marks]

05.3 Fluorine can form **ionic** bonds with metals such as sodium.

The outer shell of each atom is shown in **Figure 5.2**.

Figure 5.2

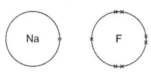

Describe what happens to the:

- electrons when an atom of sodium reacts with an atom of fluorine
- charge on the ions that form.

[4 marks]

Turn over >

06.1 Define the term **exothermic reaction**.

....

....

[1 mark]

06.2 On the sketch graph in **Figure 6.1**, draw the reaction profile of an exothermic reaction.

Label the reactants **and** the products on the profile.

Figure 6.1

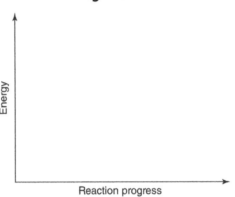

[1 mark]

06.3 Ethan is testing reactions between different chemicals that could be used in a hand warmer. **Table 6.1** shows his results.

Table 6.1

Reaction	Starting temperature (°C)	Final temperature (°C)	Temperature change (°C)
A	18	20	+2
B	19	14	
C	19	29	+10
D	20	48	+28

Calculate the temperature change for reaction B.

Temperature change for reaction B = _____ °C

[2 marks]

06.4 On the graph paper below, draw a **bar chart** for Ethan's results.

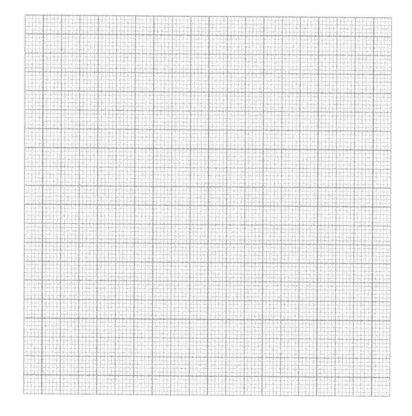

[4 marks]

Question 6 continues on the next page

06.5 When plotting results, a line graph or a bar chart might be used.

Explain why a **bar chart** was the most appropriate in this case.

....

....

[1 mark]

06.6 Using **Table 6.1** and your bar chart, suggest which reaction is **most suitable** for use in a hand warmer.

Explain why you have suggested that reaction.

Reaction ....

Explanation ....

....

....

[2 marks]

07 Figure 7.1 shows the structure of **graphene**, a substance taken from graphite.

Figure 7.1

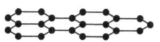

Graphene, graphite and diamond are all made up of atoms of the same element.

It is said that graphene:

- is the strongest material ever measured

- is one of the best conducting materials known

- may have the highest melting point in nature.

07.1 What single element are graphene, graphite and diamond all made from?

....

[1 mark]

07.2 Explain why **graphite** can conduct electricity, is very strong and has a high melting point.

....

....

....

....

....

....

....

....

....

....

[6 marks]

Turn over >

08   Electrolysis can be used to separate some substances into their components.

08.1 Which **two** of these substances could be separated into their components using electrolysis?

Tick **two** boxes.

Solid carbon dioxide   ☐

Molten magnesium chloride   ☐

A solution of potassium iodide ☐

Molten sulfur dioxide   ☐

Solid potassium iodide   ☐

[1 mark]

08.2 The electrolysis of sodium chloride solution (brine) can be carried out within a school laboratory or on a larger scale in industry as shown in **Figure 8.1**.

Figure 8.1

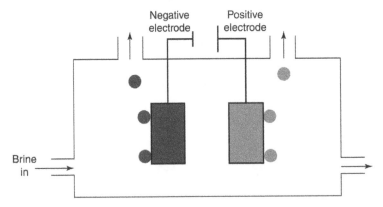

Complete **Table 8.1** to identify the name of the product formed at the positive electrode.

Table 8.1

Location	Product
positive electrode	
negative electrode	hydrogen
left in solution	sodium hydroxide

[1 mark]

08.3 Explain why hydrogen ions move to the negative electrode.

....

....

[1 mark]

08.4 Explain why hydrogen forms at the negative electrode, but sodium does not.

....

....

[1 mark]

08.5 Describe how a hydrogen ion turns into a hydrogen atom.

....

....

[1 mark]

END OF QUESTIONS

The Periodic Table

Key: Metals / Non-metals

Key to entries:
Relative atomic mass → 1
Atomic symbol → H
Name → hydrogen
Atomic/proton number → 1

1	2												3	4	5	6	7	0 or 8
								1 **H** hydrogen 1										4 **He** helium 2
7 **Li** lithium 3	9 **Be** beryllium 4												11 **B** boron 5	12 **C** carbon 6	14 **N** nitrogen 7	16 **O** oxygen 8	19 **F** fluorine 9	20 **Ne** neon 10
23 **Na** sodium 11	24 **Mg** magnesium 12												27 **Al** aluminium 13	28 **Si** silicon 14	31 **P** phosphorus 15	32 **S** sulfur 16	35.5 **Cl** chlorine 17	40 **Ar** argon 18
39 **K** potassium 19	40 **Ca** calcium 20	45 **Sc** scandium 21	48 **Ti** titanium 22	51 **V** vanadium 23	52 **Cr** chromium 24	55 **Mn** manganese 25	56 **Fe** iron 26	59 **Co** cobalt 27	59 **Ni** nickel 28	63.5 **Cu** copper 29	65 **Zn** zinc 30		70 **Ga** gallium 31	73 **Ge** germanium 32	75 **As** arsenic 33	79 **Se** selenium 34	80 **Br** bromine 35	84 **Kr** krypton 36
85 **Rb** rubidium 37	88 **Sr** strontium 38	89 **Y** yttrium 39	91 **Zr** zirconium 40	93 **Nb** niobium 41	96 **Mo** molybdenum 42	[98] **Tc** technetium 43	101 **Ru** ruthenium 44	103 **Rh** rhodium 45	106 **Pd** palladium 46	108 **Ag** silver 47	112 **Cd** cadmium 48		115 **In** indium 49	119 **Sn** tin 50	122 **Sb** antimony 51	128 **Te** tellurium 52	127 **I** iodine 53	131 **Xe** xenon 54
133 **Cs** caesium 55	137 **Ba** barium 56	139 **La*** lanthanum 57	178 **Hf** hafnium 72	181 **Ta** tantalum 73	184 **W** tungsten 74	186 **Re** rhenium 75	190 **Os** osmium 76	192 **Ir** iridium 77	195 **Pt** platinum 78	197 **Au** gold 79	201 **Hg** mercury 80		204 **Tl** thallium 81	207 **Pb** lead 82	209 **Bi** bismuth 83	[209] **Po** polonium 84	[210] **At** astatine 85	[222] **Rn** radon 86
[223] **Fr** francium 87	[226] **Ra** radium 88	[227] **Ac*** actinium 89	[261] **Rf** rutherfordium 104	[262] **Db** dubnium 105	[266] **Sg** seaborgium 106	[264] **Bh** bohrium 107	[277] **Hs** hassium 108	[268] **Mt** meitnerium 109	[271] **Ds** darmstadtium 110	[272] **Rg** roentgenium 111	[285] **Cn** copernicium 112		[286] **Uut** ununtrium 113	[289] **Fl** flerovium 114	[289] **Uup** ununpentium 115	[293] **Lv** livermorium 116	[294] **Uus** ununseptium 117	[294] **Uuo** ununoctium 118

*The lanthanides (atomic numbers 58–71) and the actinides (atomic numbers 90–103) have been omitted.

The relative atomic masses of copper and chlorine have not been rounded to the nearest whole number.

Collins

AQA
GCSE
Combined Science: Trilogy **F**
SET B – Chemistry: Paper 4 Foundation Tier
Author: Paul Lewis

Materials   Time allowed: 1 hour 15 minutes

For this paper you must have:

- a ruler
- a calculator
- the Periodic Table (found at the end of paper).

Instructions

- Answer **all** questions in the spaces provided.
- Do all rough work in this book. Cross through any work you do not want to be marked.

Information

- There are 70 marks available on this paper.
- The marks for questions are shown in brackets.
- You are expected to use a calculator where appropriate.
- You are reminded of the need for good English and clear presentation in your answers.
- When answering questions 07.3 and 08.3 you need to make sure that your answer:
  - is clear, logical, sensibly structured
  - fully meets the requirements of the question
  - shows that each separate point or step supports the overall answer.

Advice

- In all calculations, show clearly how you work out your answer.

Name: ....

01

01.1 Waste water is treated before it is returned to the fresh water cycle.

Order the stages of water treatment, 1 to 4.

Stage 3 has been done for you.

3	Anaerobic digestion of sewage sludge
	Screening and grit removal
	Aerobic biological treatment of effluent
	Sedimentation to produce sludge and effluent

[2 marks]

01.2 What is the word used for water that is safe to drink?

_____

[1 mark]

01.3 During the process of making water safe to drink, water must be sterilised.

Identify **two** ways in which water can be sterilised.

Tick **two** boxes.

Adding hydrogen ☐

Neutralisation ☐

Adding chlorine ☐

Using ultraviolet light ☐

Using microwaves ☐

[2 marks]

01.4 Water can be purified using the equipment in **Figure 1.1**.

Figure 1.1

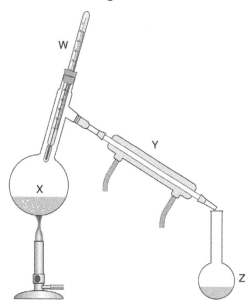

What is the name for the **whole process** involved when using this equipment?

....

[1 mark]

01.5 At which stage does **evaporation** occur?

Tick **one** box.

W ☐

X ☐

Y ☐

Z ☐

[1 mark]

Question 1 continues on the next page

01.6 At which stage does **condensation** occur?

Tick **one** box.

W ☐

X ☐

Y ☐

Z ☐

[1 mark]

02.1 **Figure 2.1** is a pie chart which shows the composition of our **current** atmosphere.

Figure 2.1

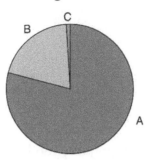

Which substance is shown by segment B in **Figure 2.1**?

Tick **one** box.

Oxygen ☐

Carbon dioxide ☐

Nitrogen ☐

Hydrogen ☐

[1 mark]

02.2 What percentage of our current atmosphere is made up of **nitrogen**?

Tick **one** box.

>1% ☐

20% ☐

79% ☐

33% ☐

[1 mark]

Question 2 continues on the next page

02.3 The amount of carbon dioxide and other greenhouse gases emitted over the life cycle of a product, service or event is called a *carbon footprint*.

State **two** ways in which we can reduce our carbon footprint.

1. ....

2. ....

[2 marks]

02.4 **Table 2.1** shows data for the changing **oxygen** levels over the last 1000 million years or so.

Table 2.1

Millions of years ago	Percentage of oxygen in the Earth's atmosphere
1000	3
800	4
600	12
400	18
200	15
0	21

Describe the changes in oxygen levels over the last 1000 million years.

....

....

....

....

....

....

[3 marks]

02.5 Explain why the levels of oxygen are different now from what they were 1000 million years ago.

....

....

....

....

[2 marks]

03 Hydrogen peroxide, H_2O_2, can decompose over time to make water and oxygen.

03.1 Write a balanced symbol equation for the decomposition of hydrogen peroxide.

....

[3 marks]

03.2 During the decomposition, oxygen gas is given off.

Describe a test that could be carried out to see if the gas is oxygen.

Describe the expected result from the test.

....

....

[2 marks]

03.3 Other chemical reactions can also give off gases.

Draw a line from each gas to the result of a positive test for that gas.

Gas	Test result
hydrogen	damp litmus paper is bleached
chlorine	limewater turns cloudy
carbon dioxide	squeaky pop is heard

[2 marks]

04 Kerosene is separated from crude oil by fractional distillation.

Figure 4.1 is a diagram of a fractional distillation column.

Figure 4.1

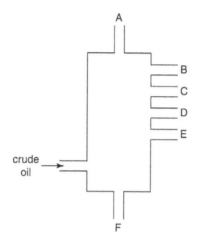

Fractional distillation allows for crude oil to be turned into useful substances.

Table 4.1 shows information about some of the useful fractions that are produced in this process.

Table 4.1

Fraction	Number of carbon atoms in the chain of the molecule	Boiling point (°C)
fuel oil	22–28	350–450
diesel	17–22	220–350
kerosene	10–16	160–220
gasoline	6–10	35–160
LPG	1–5	<35

Use **Figure 4.1** and **Table 4.1** to answer the following questions.

Question 4 continues on the next page

04.1 Order the stages of the fractional distillation of crude oil to obtain kerosene, 1 to 5.

Stage 3 has been done for you.

	Most of the crude oil evaporates and the vapours enter the column.
	Vapours that don't condense escape out the top of the column.
	Crude oil is heated to around 350 °C.
3	Crude oil that didn't evaporate runs off at the bottom of the column.
	The vapours condense at their own boiling point.

[2 marks]

04.2 Which letter on **Figure 4.1** shows where **fuel oil** is most likely to be produced?

Letter: ....

[1 mark]

04.3 Which letter on **Figure 4.1** shows where **LPG** is most likely to be produced?

Letter: ....

[1 mark]

04.4 Describe the pattern in the data between **length of carbon chain** and **boiling point of each fraction.**

....

....

[1 mark]

04.5 Explain why each fraction has a range for their boiling point, and not an exact temperature.

....

....

[1 mark]

04.6 Which of the following statements about the fractions in **Table 4.1** are correct?

Tick **two** boxes.

LPG and diesel are solids at 65 °C. ☐

Diesel and fuel oil are gases at 200 °C. ☐

LPG evaporates first when crude oil is heated. ☐

Fuel oil has the highest boiling point. ☐

[2 marks]

Turn over >

05 Scientists and food producers regularly test samples of food to identify any additives that may be in them.

Figure 5.1

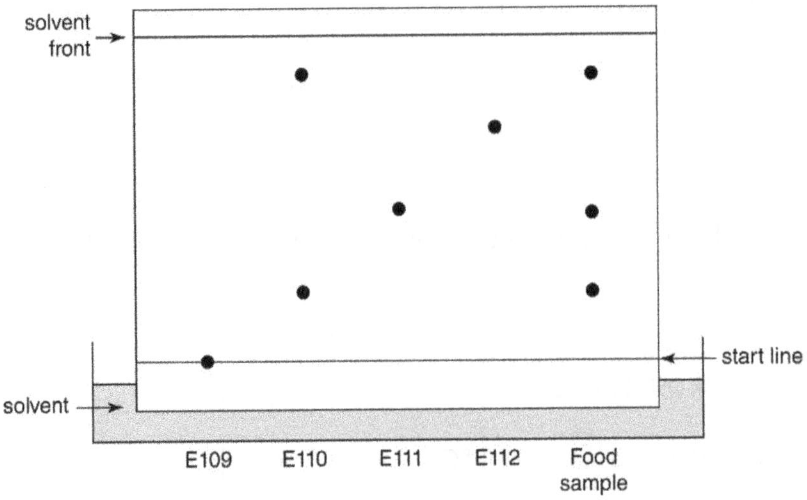

05.1 Name the analysis process used by the scientist in **Figure 5.1**.

Tick **one** box.

Chromatography ☐

Distillation ☐

Evaporation ☐

[1 mark]

05.2 For this process to work successfully the start line must be drawn correctly.

State **two** methods to ensure that the start line has been drawn correctly.

1. ....

2. ....

[2 marks]

05.3 How many colours are in the food sample?

....

[1 mark]

05.4 Which additives does the food contain?

Explain how you can tell that the food contains these additives.

Additives in the food: ....

Explanation: ....

....

[2 marks]

05.5 Explain why E109 has **not** moved from the start line.

....

....

[1 mark]

Question 5 continues on the next page

05.6 Calculate the R_f value for E112.

Use **Figure 5.1** and the equation:

$$R_f = \frac{\text{distance travelled by E112}}{\text{distance travelled by solvent front}}$$

Give your answer to two decimal places.

[4 marks]

06 A student is investigating how temperature affects the rate of a reaction.

She is investigating how the temperature of hydrochloric acid affects how quickly a strip of magnesium reacts.

This is her method:

1. Place 25 cm³ of 20 °C hydrochloric acid into a test tube.

2. Using scissors and a ruler, cut a 2 cm strip of magnesium.

3. Place the 2 cm strip of magnesium into the test tube with the acid. Start the timer.

4. When the magnesium is fully reacted, stop the timer.

5. Repeat steps 1–4 using different temperatures of hydrochloric acid.

6. Repeat the investigation so you have three sets of results for each temperature.

06.1 Identify **one** control variable in this investigation.

....

[1 mark]

06.2 One source of inaccuracy in this experiment is the length of the magnesium strip.

Suggest an alternative method that would help overcome this.

....

....

[1 mark]

Question 6 continues on the next page

06.3 The student's results are shown in **Table 6.1**.

Table 6.1

Temperature of 1 mol/dm³ hydrochloric acid (°C)	Time taken for the magnesium to react (s)			Mean time taken for the magnesium to react (s)
20	73	73	76	74
30	70	60	57	
40	37	33	36	35
50	24	26	24	25
60	14	16	13	14

Calculate the mean for the set of results at 30 °C. (Ignore any anomalies.)

....

....

Mean = ... s

[2 marks]

06.4 Plot these results on the grid below.

Draw a line of best fit.

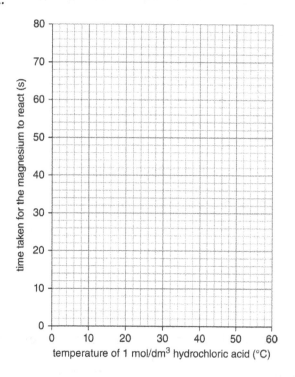

[3 marks]

Turn over >

07 Hydrocarbons, such as alkanes and alkenes, are used as fuels.

07.1 Explain the meaning of the term **hydrocarbon** by completing the sentence below.

A hydrocarbon is a substance made up of only _____ and

_____ atoms.

[2 marks]

07.2 For hydrocarbons to be used as fuels, they have to be burnt in oxygen.

What name is given to this type of reaction?

_____

[1 mark]

07.3 The shorter the hydrocarbon molecule chain, the easier it is for the fuel to burn.

Longer chained molecules can be broken into shorter chained molecules.

Substances such as decane can undergo **cracking**, in certain conditions, to be made into more useful substances that are easier to burn.

In cracking, the original (longer) alkane produces a shorter alkane and an alkene.

An equation for the cracking of decane is:

$$C_{10}H_{22} \rightarrow C_5H_{12} + C_5H_{10}$$

Describe the process of cracking decane.

Use the information above, and your own knowledge.

Your answer should include:

- the conditions needed for cracking to occur
- diagrams to show the two products produced
- a chemical test to distinguish between the two products.

_____

_____

_____

_____

_____

_____

_____

_____

_____

_____

_____

_____

_____

_____

_____

_____

[6 marks]

Turn over >

08 A student investigated the effect of changing the concentration of an acid on the rate of reaction with magnesium.

Figure 8.1 shows some of the equipment that was available.

Figure 8.1

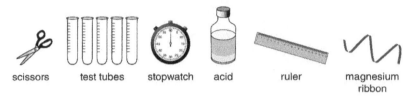

scissors   test tubes   stopwatch   acid   ruler   magnesium ribbon

Table 8.1 shows the student's results.

Table 8.1

Concentration of acid (g/dm³)	Time taken for magnesium to react (s)
0.2	226
0.4	179
0.6	114
0.8	68
1.0	23

08.1 Describe any patterns in the results shown in **Table 8.1**.

....

....

....

[2 marks]

    ©HarperCollins*Publishers* 2019

08.2 Explain, in terms of particles and collisions, why a stronger concentration affects the rate of reaction.

....

....

....

....

[3 marks]

08.3 Write a plan for the experiment which the student could have used.

Use the information above, and your own knowledge.

Your answer should include:

- a description of how to make the investigation a fair test
- a description of how to carry out the investigation safely
- a description of any measurements the student needed to take.

....

....

....

....

....

....

....

....

....

....

Continues your answer on the next page

[6 marks]

END OF QUESTIONS

BLANK PAGE

The Periodic Table

Key

Metals

Non-metals

Relative atomic mass →
Atomic symbol →
Name →
Atomic/proton number →

1		
1	**H**	hydrogen	1

1	2		3	4	5	6	7	0 or 8
								4 **He** helium 2
7 **Li** lithium 3	9 **Be** beryllium 4		11 **B** boron 5	12 **C** carbon 6	14 **N** nitrogen 7	16 **O** oxygen 8	19 **F** fluorine 9	20 **Ne** neon 10
23 **Na** sodium 11	24 **Mg** magnesium 12		27 **Al** aluminium 13	28 **Si** silicon 14	31 **P** phosphorus 15	32 **S** sulfur 16	35.5 **Cl** chlorine 17	40 **Ar** argon 18

1	2											3	4	5	6	7	0 or 8
39 **K** potassium 19	40 **Ca** calcium 20	45 **Sc** scandium 21	48 **Ti** titanium 22	51 **V** vanadium 23	52 **Cr** chromium 24	55 **Mn** manganese 25	56 **Fe** iron 26	59 **Co** cobalt 27	59 **Ni** nickel 28	63.5 **Cu** copper 29	65 **Zn** zinc 30	70 **Ga** gallium 31	73 **Ge** germanium 32	75 **As** arsenic 33	79 **Se** selenium 34	80 **Br** bromine 35	84 **Kr** krypton 36
85 **Rb** rubidium 37	88 **Sr** strontium 38	89 **Y** yttrium 39	91 **Zr** zirconium 40	93 **Nb** niobium 41	96 **Mo** molybdenum 42	[98] **Tc** technetium 43	101 **Ru** ruthenium 44	103 **Rh** rhodium 45	106 **Pd** palladium 46	108 **Ag** silver 47	112 **Cd** cadmium 48	115 **In** indium 49	119 **Sn** tin 50	122 **Sb** antimony 51	128 **Te** tellurium 52	127 **I** iodine 53	131 **Xe** xenon 54
133 **Cs** caesium 55	137 **Ba** barium 56	139 **La*** lanthanum 57	178 **Hf** hafnium 72	181 **Ta** tantalum 73	184 **W** tungsten 74	186 **Re** rhenium 75	190 **Os** osmium 76	192 **Ir** iridium 77	195 **Pt** platinum 78	197 **Au** gold 79	201 **Hg** mercury 80	204 **Tl** thallium 81	207 **Pb** lead 82	209 **Bi** bismuth 83	[209] **Po** polonium 84	[210] **At** astatine 85	[222] **Rn** radon 86
[223] **Fr** francium 87	[226] **Ra** radium 88	[227] **Ac*** actinium 89	[261] **Rf** rutherfordium 104	[262] **Db** dubnium 105	[266] **Sg** seaborgium 106	[264] **Bh** bohrium 107	[277] **Hs** hassium 108	[268] **Mt** meitnerium 109	[271] **Ds** darmstadtium 110	[272] **Rg** roentgenium 111	[285] **Cn** copernicium 112	[286] **Uut** ununtrium 113	[289] **Fl** flerovium 114	[289] **Uup** ununpentium 115	[293] **Lv** livermorium 116	[294] **Uus** ununseptium 117	[294] **Uuo** ununoctium 118

*The lanthanides (atomic numbers 58–71) and the actinides (atomic numbers 90–103) have been omitted.
The relative atomic masses of copper and chlorine have not been rounded to the nearest whole number.

Collins

AQA
GCSE
Combined Science: Trilogy   F
SET B – Physics: Paper 5 Foundation Tier
Author: Lynn Pharaoh

Materials   Time allowed: 1 hour 15 minutes

For this paper you must have:
- a ruler
- a calculator
- the Physics Equation Sheet (found at the end of the paper).

Instructions

- Answer all questions in the spaces provided.
- Do all rough work in this book. Cross through any work you do not want to be marked.

Information

- There are 70 marks available on this paper.
- The marks for questions are shown in brackets.
- You are expected to use a calculator where appropriate.
- You are reminded of the need for good English and clear presentation in your answers.
- When answering questions 03.1 and 09.1 you need to make sure that your answer:
  – is clear, logical, sensibly structured
  – fully meets the requirements of the question
  – shows that each separate point or step supports the overall answer.

Advice

- In all calculations, show clearly how you work out your answer.

Name: ....

01

01.1 Which type of nuclear radiation has the **greatest ionising power**?

Tick **one** box.

Alpha ☐

Beta ☐

Gamma ☐

[1 mark]

01.2 Which type of nuclear radiation has the **shortest range in air**?

Tick **one** box.

Alpha ☐

Beta ☐

Gamma ☐

[1 mark]

01.3 Which type of nuclear radiation consists of **high speed electrons**?

Tick **one** box.

Alpha ☐

Beta ☐

Gamma ☐

[1 mark]

01.4 Which type of nuclear radiation does **not** consist of **charged particles**?

Tick **one** box.

Alpha ☐

Beta ☐

Gamma ☐

[1 mark]

01.5 Which type of radiation does **not** cause the **mass of the nucleus** from which it is emitted to **change**?

Tick **one** box.

Alpha ☐

Beta ☐

Gamma ☐

[1 mark]

01.6 Which type of radiation is emitted when a **neutron** inside a nucleus **changes into a proton**?

Tick **one** box.

Alpha ☐

Beta ☐

Gamma ☐

[1 mark]

Turn over >

02   A student sets up a circuit to measure current and potential difference values for an unknown electrical component.

Figure 2.1 shows the component marked with an 'X'.

Figure 2.1

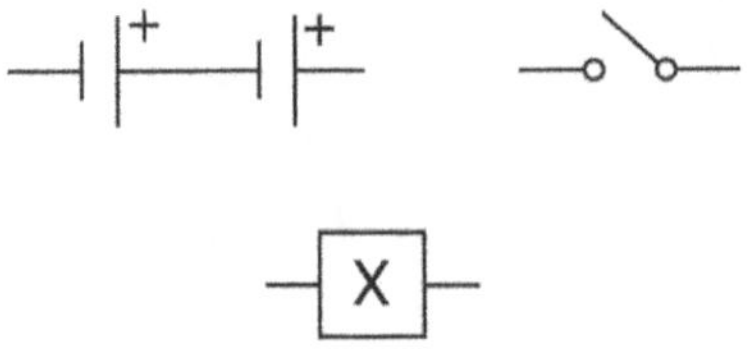

02.1 Complete the circuit diagram to show a circuit that could be used to take several **different** measurements of current through X and potential difference across X.

[3 marks]

02.2 The student sets up the circuit so that the current from the battery is 0.12 A

Calculate the charge that flows through component X in 10 s

Use the following equation:

charge = current × time

Give the correct unit with your answer.

Charge = ...

Unit: ....

[3 marks]

02.3 **Figure 2.2** is a graph of the student's current and potential difference measurements for component X.

Figure 2.2

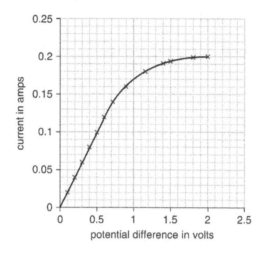

Use **Figure 2.2** to give **two** conclusions about component X.

....

....

....

....

[2 marks]

Turn over >

03

03.1 Experiments during the late 19th century and the early 20th century enabled scientists to develop the model of the atom. They replaced the **plum pudding model** with the **nuclear model**.

Compare the main features of the plum pudding model and the nuclear model of the atom.

....

....

....

....

....

....

....

....

....

....

[4 marks]

03.2 Further experiments showed that the atomic nucleus consists of two types of particle.

Name the **two** types of particle found in the nucleus.

1. ....

2. ....

[2 marks]

04.1 Explain what is meant by an **isotope**.

....

....

[1 mark]

04.2 A nucleus of an isotope of radon, $^{222}_{86}$Rn, undergoes radioactive decay by alpha emission to form a nucleus of polonium, Po.

Complete the nuclear equation showing the decay of radon.

Add the **two** missing numbers to the equation.

$$^{222}_{86}\text{Rn} \rightarrow {}^{218}_{\square}\text{Po} + {}^{\square}_{2}\text{He}$$

[2 marks]

04.3 The polonium-218 nucleus undergoes radioactive decay by beta emission.

Complete the nuclear equation showing the decay of polonium-218 by beta emission.

Add the **three** missing numbers to the equation.

$$^{218}_{84}\text{Po} \rightarrow {}^{\square}_{\square}\text{At} + {}^{0}_{\square}\text{e}$$

[3 marks]

Turn over >

05.1 **Table 5.1** shows the typical power of some household electrical appliances.

Table 5.1

Appliance	Hair dryer	Laptop	Iron	Printer	Electric kettle
Power in W	1800	60	1000	25	2000

What do the **three** most powerful appliances have in common?

....

[1 mark]

05.2 Which appliance in **Table 5.1** transfers energy at the **slowest** rate?

....

[1 mark]

05.3 In UK homes, the cables that connect a mains socket to an appliance usually contain three wires. Each wire has its own colour scheme.

Draw a line from each wire to its colour scheme.

Wire		**Colour scheme**

Live
Neutral
Earth

Blue
Green and yellow stripes
Brown

[2 marks]

05.4 Which wire prevents the appliance from becoming live if there is a fault?

Tick **one** box.

Live ☐

Neutral ☐

Earth ☐

[1 mark]

05.5 Which wire carries the alternating potential difference from the mains supply?

Tick **one** box.

Live ☐

Neutral ☐

Earth ☐

[1 mark]

05.6 Write down the equation that links power, current and resistance.

....

[1 mark]

05.7 A lawnmower is connected through an extension cable to the mains.

The resistance of the cable is 2.0 Ω

The current in the cable is 4.0 A

Calculate the power wasted as heat in the extension cable when the lawnmower is being used.

....

Power = ... W

[2 marks]

Turn over >

06 A system is an object or a group of objects. The way energy is stored in a system can change when the system changes.

06.1 Draw a line from each system change to the correct energy store change.

System change	Energy store change
	Gravitational potential energy to kinetic energy
A cup of tea cooling down	Elastic potential energy to thermal energy
A falling football	Thermal energy dissipated to the surroundings
A car braking	Kinetic energy to thermal energy

[3 marks]

06.2 A student attaches a weight to a spring, causing the spring to stretch.

Name the energy store associated with the stretched spring.

....

[1 mark]

06.3 The weight extends the spring by 0.12 m

The spring constant of the spring is 25 N/m

Calculate the amount of energy stored in the spring.

Select the correct equation from the Physics Equation Sheet.

....

....

Energy stored = ... J

[2 marks]

07.1 Name component Q in **Figure 7.1**.

_____

Figure 7.1

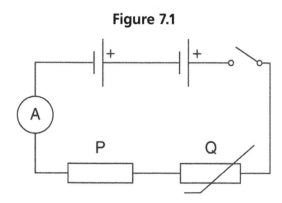

[1 mark]

07.2 **Figure 7.2** shows how the resistance of component Q changes as its temperature is changed.

Figure 7.2

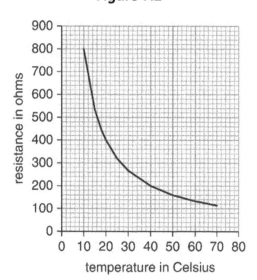

Describe the trend shown by **Figure 7.2**.

_____

_____

[1 mark]

Question 7 continues on the next page

07.3 How would the reading of the ammeter in **Figure 7.1** change if the temperature of component Q increased?

Explain your answer.

....

....

....

[2 marks]

07.4 Use **Figure 7.2** to determine the resistance of component Q at a temperature of 20°C.

Resistance = ... Ω

[1 mark]

07.5 Component P in **Figure 7.1** is a fixed resistor with a resistance of 800 Ω

Calculate the **total resistance** in the circuit when component Q is at 20°C

....

Total resistance .... Ω

[1 mark]

07.6 Write down the equation that links potential difference, current and resistance.

....

[1 mark]

07.7 The battery in **Figure 7.1** supplies a 6.0 V potential difference.

Calculate the current through the ammeter when component Q is at 20°C

....

....

....

Current = ... A

[3 marks]

08 **Figure 8.1** shows an aluminium block being heated by an electric immersion heater.

Figure 8.1

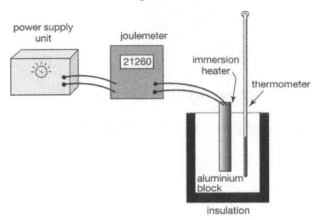

08.1 A student intends to heat the aluminium block and measure its temperature before and after heating.

The temperature of the block is expected to rise by approximately 20°C

The room temperature of the laboratory is 18°C

Table 8.1 shows some thermometers that are available.

Table 8.1

Thermometer	Range in °C	Value of one division in °C
A	−10 to 110	1
B	34 to 44	0.1
C	−10 to 50	0.5
D	−10 to 200	2

Which is the most suitable thermometer for the student's measurements?

Explain your answer.

....

....

....

....

[3 marks]

08.2 The student's measurements are shown in **Table 8.2**.

The energy supplied to the block is measured by the joulemeter shown in **Figure 8.1**.

Table 8.2

Measurement	Value
Mass of block	1.00 kg
Initial temperature of the block	18.5°C
Energy supplied	21260 J
Final temperature of the block	41.5°C

Determine the temperature rise of the aluminium block.

Temperature rise = ... °C

[1 mark]

08.3 Use the student's data from **Table 8.2** to calculate the **specific heat capacity** of aluminium.

Use the correct equation from the Physics Equation Sheet.

Give your answer to 3 significant figures.

Specific heat capacity = ... J/kg °C

[4 marks]

Question 8 continues on the next page

08.4 The student then uses the same apparatus in **Figure 8.1** to compare the energy needed to raise the temperature of blocks of **different** materials.

The readings for each block are shown in **Table 8.3**.

Table 8.3

Metal block	Mass in kg	Thermal energy in J supplied	Temperature rise in °C
Cast iron	1.00	4701	10
Brass	1.00	3850	10
Nickel	1.00	4512	10
Aluminium	1.00	8970	10

Which metal block in **Table 8.3** would need the most energy to raise its temperature by 1°C?

....

[1 mark]

08.5 Which metal in **Table 8.3** has the **highest specific heat capacity**?

....

[1 mark]

08.6 Which metal in **Table 8.3** has the **lowest specific heat capacity**?

....

[1 mark]

09.1 A student wants to measure the density of cooking oil.

Write a plan for the student to follow.

Name any apparatus that will be needed.

[6 marks]

Question 9 continues on the next page

09.2 The student wants to reduce the effect of **random errors** on his density value for cooking oil.

Suggest what he should do.

....

....

....

[2 marks]

END OF QUESTIONS

BLANK PAGE

Physics Equation Sheet

Equation Number	Word Equation	Symbol Equation
1	(final velocity)^2 – (initial velocity)^2 = 2 × acceleration × distance	$v^2 - u^2 = 2\,a\,s$
2	elastic potential energy = 0.5 × spring constant × (extension)^2	$E_e = \dfrac{1}{2}\,k\,e^2$
3	change in thermal energy = mass × specific heat capacity × temperature change	$\Delta E = m\,c\,\Delta\theta$
4	period = $\dfrac{1}{\text{frequency}}$	
5	thermal energy for a change of state = mass × specific latent heat	$E = mL$

©HarperCollins*Publishers* 2019

Collins

AQA
GCSE

Combined Science: Trilogy　F

SET B – Physics: Paper 6 Foundation Tier

Author: Lynn Pharaoh

Materials　　　　　　　　　　　　　　　Time allowed: 1 hour 15 minutes

For this paper you must have:

- a ruler
- a calculator
- the Physics Equation Sheet (found at the end of the paper).

Instructions

- Answer all questions in the spaces provided.
- Do all rough work in this book. Cross through any work you do not want to be marked.

Information

- There are 70 marks available on this paper.
- The marks for questions are shown in brackets.
- You are expected to use a calculator where appropriate.
- You are reminded of the need for good English and clear presentation in your answers.
- When answering question 07.2 you need to make sure that your answer:
  – is clear, logical, sensibly structured
  – fully meets the requirements of the question
  – shows that each separate point or step supports the overall answer.

Advice

- In all calculations, show clearly how you work out your answer.

Name: ....

01   **Figure 1.1** shows the groups of waves in the electromagnetic spectrum.

Figure 1.1

Radio waves	Microwaves	Infrared	Visible light	Ultraviolet	X-rays	Gamma waves

01.1 Which group of waves in the electromagnetic spectrum has the **shortest wavelength**?

....

[1 mark]

01.2 Which group of waves in the electromagnetic spectrum **causes a sun tan**?

....

[1 mark]

01.3 Which group of waves in the electromagnetic spectrum **originates in the nucleus of atoms**?

....

[1 mark]

01.4 Which **two** groups of waves in the electromagnetic spectrum are used for **transferring thermal energy** during the cooking of food?

1. ....

2. ....

[2 marks]

01.5 Which group of waves in the electromagnetic spectrum can **cause skin to age prematurely**?

....

[1 mark]

01.6 Which group of waves in the electromagnetic spectrum is used for **transmitting satellite TV channels**?

....

[1 mark]

01.7 **Table 1.1** shows information about doses and risks of some X-ray procedures.

Table 1.1

X-ray procedure	Typical dose in mSv	Equivalent period of background radiation	Lifetime additional risk of fatal cancer
teeth	0.01	1.5 days	1 in 2 million
chest	0.02	3 days	1 in a million
skull	0.07	11 days	1 in 300 000
neck	0.08	2 weeks	1 in 200 000

[Data from Public Health England]

Suggest **two** conclusions that can be made from the data in **Table 1.1**.

1. ....

....

2. ....

....

[2 marks]

Turn over >

02

02.1 Explain the difference between the terms **speed** and **velocity**.

....

....

[1 mark]

02.2 What is a typical speed for a person walking?

Tick **one** box.

1.5 m/s ☐

8 m/s ☐

20 m/s ☐

[1 mark]

02.3 The graph in **Figure 2.1** shows the motion of a car on a straight track.

Figure 2.1

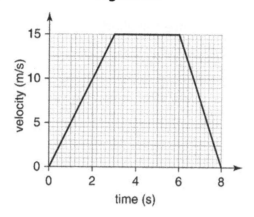

Give **three** descriptions of the motion of the car shown in **Figure 2.1**.

1. ....

   ....

2. ....

   ....

3. ....

   ....

[3 marks]

Question 2 continues on the next page

02.4 An aircraft is flying at a speed of 90 m/s

Use the following equation to calculate distance travelled by the aircraft in 1 minute.

distance travelled = speed × time

Distance travelled = _____ m

[3 marks]

03 A car driver approaches a hazard.

03.1 Explain what is meant by the **thinking distance**.

....

....

[1 mark]

03.2 Write down **one** factor that can affect the thinking distance.

....

[1 mark]

03.3 Explain what is meant by the **braking distance**.

....

....

[1 mark]

03.4 Write down **one** factor that can affect the braking distance.

....

[1 mark]

03.5 Which energy transfer occurs when the brakes of a moving car are applied?

Tick **one** box.

Chemical energy to kinetic energy ☐

Gravitational potential energy to thermal energy ☐

Kinetic energy to thermal energy ☐

[1 mark]

Question 3 continues on the next page

03.6 Write down **one** effect that the energy transfer has on the car's brakes.

....

....

[1 mark]

03.7 Figure 3.1 shows changes in thinking distance and braking distance with car speed.

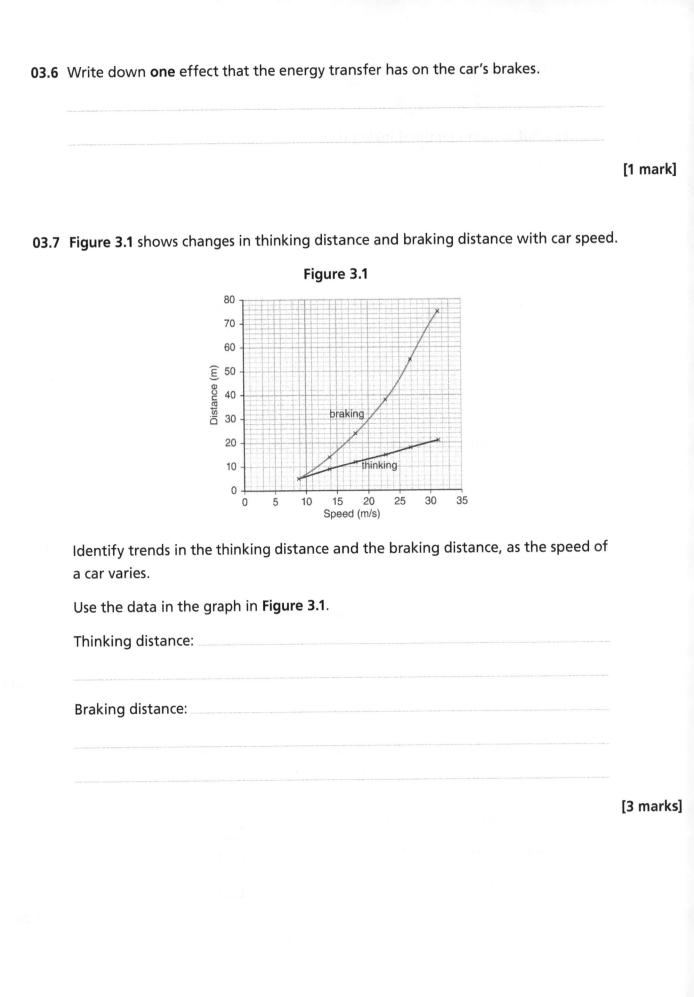

Figure 3.1

Identify trends in the thinking distance and the braking distance, as the speed of a car varies.

Use the data in the graph in **Figure 3.1**.

Thinking distance: ....

....

Braking distance: ....

....

....

[3 marks]

04.1 The book in **Figure 4.1** is at rest on the bench.

Figure 4.1

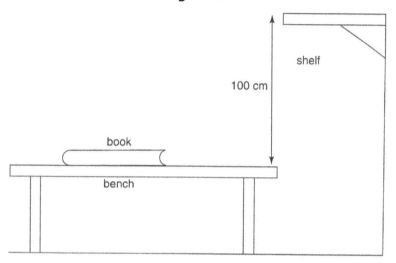

The weight of the book is the force of gravity exerted on the book by the Earth.

Complete the following sentences.

Choose words from the box.

First	Second	Third	mass
Earth	contact	non-contact	weight

According to Newton's .... Law, the bench exerts a force on the
book equal in size to the book's ....

The force of gravity is a type of .... force.

[3 marks]

04.2 Write down the equation that links weight, mass and gravitational field strength.

....

[1 mark]

Question 4 continues on the next page

04.3 The book on the bench in **Figure 4.1** has a mass of 500 g

Calculate the weight of the book.

Gravitational field strength = 9.8 N/kg

Weight = ... N

[3 marks]

04.4 Write down the equation that links work done, force and distance moved.

....

[1 mark]

04.5 A person lifts the book the distance of 100 cm to put the book on the shelf.

Calculate the work done by the person in putting the book on to the shelf.

Give the unit for your answer.

....

Work done = ...

Unit ....

[3 marks]

05 **Figure 5.1** is a snapshot of a wave on a rope.

One end of the rope is attached to a wall.

The other end of the rope is moved up and down by hand.

Figure 5.1

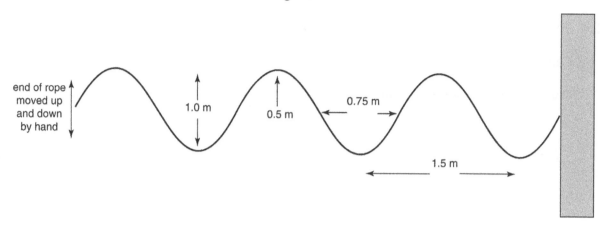

05.1 What is the wavelength of the wave on the rope in **Figure 5.1**?

Tick **one** box.

0.5 m ☐

0.75 m ☐

1.0 m ☐

1.5 m ☐

[1 mark]

05.2 What **type** of wave is travelling on the rope?

_____

[1 mark]

Question 5 continues on the next page

05.3 Write down the equation that links wave speed, frequency and wavelength.

....

[1 mark]

05.4 30 waves are produced on the rope in 15 s

Calculate the wave speed.

Give the unit for your answer.

....

....

....

Wave speed = ...

Unit ....

[4 marks]

06 A student is investigating how the size of the force accelerating an object affects the acceleration, assuming the object's mass stays constant.

The student uses the air track and glider shown in **Figure 6.1**.

Figure 6.1

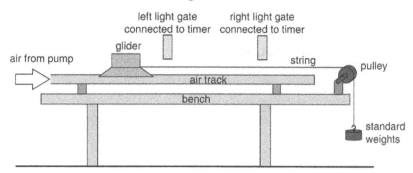

06.1 Identify the **independent**, the **dependent** and **one control** variable in this investigation.

Independent variable: ....

Dependent variable: ....

Control variable: ....

[3 marks]

06.2 What creates the force that accelerates the glider?

....

[1 mark]

06.3 Air is pumped into the air track, lifting the glider up from the track slightly.

What effect would you expect this to have on the motion of the glider?

Explain your answer.

....

....

[2 marks]

Question 6 continues on the next page

06.4 One set of the student's measurements is shown in **Table 6.1**.

Table 6.1

Velocity through left light gate	0.10 m/s
Velocity through right light gate	0.20 m/s
Gate separation	0.50 m
Force (accelerating the glider)	0.015 N

Use the following equation to calculate the glider's acceleration.

$$\text{acceleration} = \frac{(\text{final velocity})^2 - (\text{initial velocity})^2}{(2 \times \text{gate separation})}$$

Acceleration = ... m/s²

[2 marks]

06.5 The student obtains four more sets of acceleration and force data for the glider.

The data is shown in **Table 6.2**.

Table 6.2

Force accelerating the glider in N	Acceleration in m/s²
0.020	0.040
0.030	0.060
0.040	0.080
0.050	0.100

The student concludes that increasing the force increases the acceleration of the glider.

What other conclusion can be made from **Table 6.2** about the relationship between force and acceleration of the air track glider?

....

....

[1 mark]

©HarperCollins*Publishers* 2019

06.6 Write down the equation that links resultant force, mass and acceleration.

....

[1 mark]

06.7 Calculate the mass of the glider.

Use data from **Table 6.2**.

Assume that the force accelerating the glider is the resultant force on the glider.

....

....

Mass of glider = ... kg

[3 marks]

07   **Figure 7.1** shows an electromagnet made by a student.

The iron core is clamped vertically.

Figure 7.1

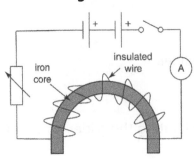

07.1 The student also has an iron nail.

Describe how the student can use this to show that the electromagnet's iron core is only magnetised when there is a current in the wire.

....

....

....

[2 marks]

7.2   The student wants to measure the strength of her electromagnet.

She uses an iron bar and known masses on a mass hanger, as shown in **Figure 7.2**. The iron bar is attracted to the electromagnet.

The student gradually adds masses to the hanger.

When the total weight is large enough to overcome the attractive force exerted by the electromagnet, the iron bar and the masses fall to the ground.

Figure 7.2

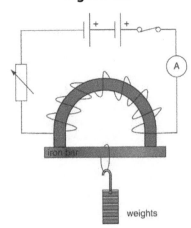

The student wants to investigate how the size of the current in the wire affects the attractive force exerted by the electromagnet.

Write step-by-step instructions for the student to follow, using apparatus in **Figure 7.2**.

Include any safety precautions needed.

Include a procedure to ensure accurate data is obtained.

_____

_____

_____

_____

_____

_____

_____

_____

_____

_____

_____

_____

[6 marks]

Question 7 continues on the next page

07.3 The student records the measurements shown in **Table 7.1.**

Table 7.1

| Current in A | Total weight supported by electromagnet in N | | |
	Measurement 1	Measurement 2	Mean
0.5	1.0	1.0	1.0
1.0	2.2	2.0	2.1
1.5	3.0	3.2	3.1
2.0	4.2	4.2	
2.5	5.1	5.3	

Complete the **mean total weight** column of **Table 7.1**.

[1 mark]

07.4 **Figure 7.3** is a graph to show how the total weight supported by the electromagnet depends on the current in the coil.

Figure 7.3

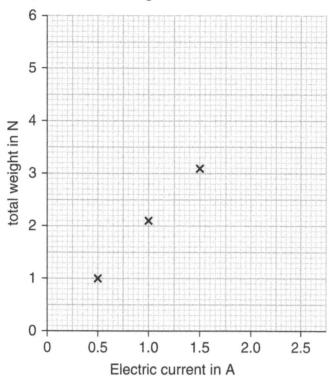

Three data points have been plotted but the graph is incomplete.

Plot the remaining points, using your completed **Table 7.1**.

Draw a line of best fit.

[2 marks]

07.5 Write a conclusion about how the size of the electric current in the wire affects the strength of the electromagnet.

Use data from the graph in **Figure 7.3**.

....

....

....

[2 marks]

END OF QUESTIONS

Physics Equation Sheet

Equation Number	Word Equation	Symbol Equation
1	(final velocity)^2 – (initial velocity)^2 = 2 × acceleration × distance	$v^2 - u^2 = 2\,a\,s$
2	elastic potential energy = 0.5 × spring constant × (extension)^2	$E_e = \dfrac{1}{2}\,k\,e^2$
3	change in thermal energy = mass × specific heat capacity × temperature change	$\Delta E = m\,c\,\Delta\Theta$
4	period = $\dfrac{1}{\text{frequency}}$	
5	thermal energy for a change of state = mass × specific latent heat	$E = mL$

Answers

Set A – Biology: Paper 1

Question	Answer(s)	Extra info	Mark(s)	AO/Spec ref.
01.1	B any **one** from: • axon / long fibre • nerve endings • cell body • sheath		1 1	AO1 4.1.1.3
01.2	C projection / hair	allow is the only plant cell or point that implies this e.g. it is the only one with a cell wall/large vacuole	1 1	AO1 4.1.1.3
01.3	A tail	allow can swim	1 1	AO1 4.1.1.3
01.4	C has a cell wall	allow is a root hair cell allow has a large vacuole	1 1	AO1 4.1.1.2
02.1	oxygen		1	AO1 4.4.1.1
02.2	palisade mesophyll		1	AO1 4.2.3.1
02.3	$C_6H_{12}O_6$		1	AO1 4.4.1.1
02.4	Amino acids → Protein synthesis Cellulose → Strengthen cell walls Starch → Food storage all three correct for **2 marks** one or two correct for **1 mark**	each extra line negates a mark	2	AO1 4.4.1.3
02.5	phloem translocation	in this order only	1 1	AO1 4.2.3.2
02.6	midday it is warmer the light is brighter	allow the stomata are fully open	1 1 1	AO2/ AO3 4.4.1.2
03.1	Plasma → Carry dissolved food and other substances around the body Platelets → Form blood clots White blood cells → Protect the body against infection all three correct for **2 marks** one or two correct for **1 mark**	each extra line negates a mark	2	AO1 4.2.2.3
03.2	more likely to become infected **or** less able to defend against pathogens		1	AO2 4.3.1.6
03.3	Artery, Capillary, Vein (matched to diagrams) all three correct for **2 marks** one or two correct for **1 mark**	each extra line negates a mark	2	AO1 4.2.2.2
03.4	less oxygen/glucose gets to heart muscle heart muscle respires less / works less efficiently		1 1	AO1/ AO2 4.2.2.4 4.4.2.1
03.5	artificial heart this will keep the patient alive until donor heart available		1 1	AO3 4.2.2.4
04.1	blocks oxygen/air from the water **or** stops larva/pupa breathing **or** prevents mosquitoes laying eggs **or** hampers adult emerging reduces risk of being bitten by mosquito / transmission of malarial parasite		1 1	AO2 4.3.1.5
04.2	they are unlikely to bite someone with malaria so they do not carry/transmit *Plasmodium* (if they bite someone else)		1 1	AO3 4.3.1.5
04.3	Measles → Viral Rose black spot → Fungal Salmonella food poisoning → Bacterial all three correct for **2 marks** one or two correct for **1 mark**	each extra line negates a mark	2	AO1 4.3.1.2 4.3.1.3 4.3.1.4
04.4	it has a nucleus it does not have a cell wall	allow it does not have plasmids allow DNA is not in a loop allow it does not have a (slime) capsule	1 1	AO2 4.1.1.1
05.1	fermentation		1	AO1 4.4.2.1
05.2	keep out oxygen so yeast does anaerobic respiration **or** so yeast cannot use aerobic respiration		1 1	AO2 4.4.2.1

Question	Answer(s)	Extra info	Mark(s)	AO/Spec ref.
05.3	to allow carbon dioxide to escape		1	AO2 4.4.2.1
	otherwise pressure will build up		1	
05.4	glucose → lactic acid	all correct for **2 marks** allow **1 mark** if glucose shown as reactant **or** lactic acid shown as product deduct mark for each additional incorrect reactant or product (e.g. oxygen, carbon dioxide) allow correct symbols in place of glucose or lactic acid	2	AO1 4.4.2.1
05.5	any one from: • lactic acid causes fatigue/aches • anaerobic respiration transfers less energy than aerobic respiration • lactic acid is toxic if it builds up in the body		1	AO2 4.4.2.1 4.4.2.2 4.4.2.1
06.1	(medicines like aspirin) are painkillers / treat the symptoms		1	AO2 4.3.1.8
	(antibiotics) do not kill viruses		1	
06.2	any two from: • test for toxicity/safety • test for efficacy / effectiveness • test to find best dose		2	AO1 4.3.1.9
06.3	**Level 2:** a detailed and coherent argument is given, which explains why placebos should be used with healthy volunteers but not ill patients.		3–4	AO3 4.3.1.9
	Level 1: discrete relevant points are made, although the arguments may not be clear.		1–2	
	No relevant content		0	

Question	Answer(s)	Extra info	Mark(s)	AO/Spec ref.
	Indicative content • a placebo is a treatment that does not contain the (active) medicine/drug • placebos are used with a control group to compare with the group taking the medicine/drug • placebos can be used with healthy volunteers • placebos should not be used with ill patients • if ill patients took placebos they would not be getting any treatment • trials involving ill patients should use currently available medicines/drugs for the control group			
06.4	to avoid bias	allow so that neither doctors nor participants know who has received the (active) medicine/ drug (until the trial is completed)	1	AO2 4.3.1.9
07.1	in order: virus, red blood cell, ant, acorn all correct for **2 marks** allow **1 mark** if three are in the correct order		2	AO2 4.1.1.1
07.2	60 mm = 60 000 μm magnification = 60 000 ÷ 12 = 5000	allow 5000 with no working shown for **3 marks** allow equivalent marking points if 12 μm is converted to 0.012 mm	1 1 1	AO2 4.1.1.5
07.3	to make the structures more visible		1	AO1 4.1.1.2
	to have a large field of view / to see the layout of cells / easier to locate cells		1	
08.1	all points correctly plotted **2 marks** **but** three or four points correctly plotted **1 mark** anomalous result (25 mm) circled straight line of best fit through all points except anomalous result	allow ± half a small square	2 1 1	AO2/ AO3 4.2.3.2
08.2	as water evaporated/transpired from the leaves, water was pulled through the capillary tube (moving the air bubble)		1	AO2 4.2.3.2

Question	Answer(s)	Extra info	Mark(s)	AO/Spec ref.
08.3	**Level 3:** a coherent method is described with relevant detail, which demonstrates a broad understanding of the relevant scientific techniques and procedures. The steps in the method are logically ordered. The method would lead to the collection of valid results.		5–6	**AO3** 4.2.3.2
	Level 2: the bulk of a method is described with mostly relevant detail, which demonstrates a reasonable understanding of the relevant techniques and procedures. The method may not be in a completely logical sequence and may be missing some detail.		3–4	
	Level 1: discrete relevant points are made which demonstrate some understanding of the relevant scientific techniques and procedures. They may lack a logical structure and would not lead to the production of valid results.		1–2	
	No relevant content		0	
	Indicative content • independent variable is air movement • air movement varied by altering the speed of the fan/distance of fan from plant • dependent variable is distance bubble moves in a given time **or** time for bubble to move a given distance • control variables include: same plant, temperature, light intensity, humidity • repeat readings and calculate means			

Set A – Biology: Paper 2

Question	Answer(s)	Extra info	Mark(s)	AO/Spec ref.
01.1	**X** = pituitary **Y** = pancreas **Z** = adrenal		1 1 1	**AO1** 4.5.3.1
01.2	in the blood (system)		1	**AO1** 4.5.3.1
01.3	Insulin — Ovary Oestrogen — Testis Testosterone — Pancreas all three correct for **2** marks one or two correct for **1** mark	each extra line negates a mark	2	**AO1** 4.5.3.2 4.5.3.3
01.4	(type 1) diabetes		1	**AO1** 4.5.3.2

Question	Answer(s)	Extra info	Mark(s)	AO/Spec ref.
02.1	Arctic willow/grass		1	**AO2** 4.7.2.1
02.2	Arctic fox/snowy owl		1	**AO2** 4.7.2.1
02.3	the number would increase they have more food/Arctic hares to eat **or** there is less competition for food (with the Arctic foxes)		1 1	**AO3** 4.7.1.1
02.4	community		1	**AO1** 4.7.11
02.5	mates		1	**AO1** 4.7.1.1
02.6	any **one** adaptation with corresponding explanation: sharp/pointed teeth; to catch prey sharp/pointed claws; to catch prey eyes at front of head; binocular vision/judge distance white fur; camouflage	only award explanation mark if it matches with the adaptation	2	**AO2** 4.7.1.4
02.7	any **one** adaptation with corresponding explanation: eyes at side of head; wide field of view large ears; hear predators white fur; camouflage long legs; escape from predators	only award explanation mark if it matches with the adaptation	2	**AO2** 4.7.1.4
03.1	FSH — Causes eggs to mature LH — Maintains uterus lining Progesterone — Stimulates the release of eggs all three correct for **2** marks one or two correct for **1** mark	each extra line negates a mark	2	**AO1** 4.5.3.3

Question	Answer(s)	Extra info	Mark(s)	AO/Spec ref.
03.2	**Type of cell** / **Number of chromosomes in cell**: Sperm 23, Egg 23, Fertilised egg 46, Embryo 46 all three correct for **2 marks** one or two correct for **1 mark**		2	AO2 4.6.1.2
03.3	differentiation		1	AO1 4.6.1.2
03.4	Diaphragm — Kills sperm Intrauterine device — Prevents fertilised egg implanting Oral contraceptive — Prevents eggs maturing Spermicide — Prevents sperm reaching egg all four correct for **3 marks** two or three correct for **2 marks** one correct for **1 mark**	each extra line negates a mark	3	AO1 4.5.3.4
04.1	$100 - 13 - 4 - 9 - 58$ $= 16$ (%)	allow 16 (%) with no working shown for **2 marks**	1 1	AO2 4.7.3.5
04.2	emissions from power stations burning fossil fuels/oil/coal/(natural) gas		1 1	AO1 4.7.2.2
04.3	industrial sector – no mark on own jet fuel produces 20% of 58% = 12%	allow industrial sector because jet fuel produces 12 (%) with no working shown for **2 marks**	1 1	AO2 4.7.3.5

Question	Answer(s)	Extra info	Mark(s)	AO/Spec ref.
04.4	global warming	allow increased greenhouse effect allow description of consequences of global warming, e.g. flooding/drought/famine/climate change	1	AO1 4.7.3.5
04.5	photosynthesis		1	AO1 4.7.2.2
05.1	scar		1	AO2 4.6.2.1
05.2	DNA double helix chromosome	in this order only	1 1 1	AO1 4.6.1.3
05.3	Punnett square: A×A = AA, A×a = Aa, a×A = Aa, a×a = aa all three correct for **2 marks** one or two correct for **1 mark**		2	AO2 4.6.1.4
05.4	wet (earwax)		1	AO2 4.6.1.4
05.5	heterozygous		1	AO2 4.6.1.4
06.1	select a male and female with more meat than others breed these together from their offspring select those with most meat use these for breeding repeat over many generations		1 1 1 1 1	AO1 4.6.2.3
06.2	large udder to produce more milk **OR** smaller horns to avoid harm to farmer		2	AO2 4.6.2.3
06.3	genetic engineering		1	AO1 4.6.2.4
07.1	0		1	AO2 4.7.2.1
07.2	4		1	AO2 4.7.2.1

Question	Answer(s)	Extra info	Mark(s)	AO/Spec ref.
07.3	all points correctly plotted **3 marks** **but** at least 10 points correctly plotted **2 marks** **but** at least six points correctly plotted **1 mark** points joined up to make a 'kite'	allow ± half a small square	3 1	AO2 4.7.2.1
07.4	**Level 2:** a detailed and coherent argument is given, which explains why species B and D are more common on the path and why species A and C are more common away from the path.		3-4	AO3 4.7.1.1 4.7.2.1
	Level 1: discrete relevant points are made, although the arguments may not be clear.		1-2	
	No relevant content		0	
	Indicative content • species A and C are tall(er) • species A and C are killed by mowing on the path • species A and C can survive away from the path as they are tall enough to successfully compete for light • species B and D are low-growing • species B and D are not killed by mowing on the path/are missed by the mower • species B and D cannot survive away from the path as they are not tall enough to successfully compete for light			
08.1	**Level 3:** a coherent evaluation is given, with relevant details, which demonstrates an understanding of the principles of investigations and analysis of results.		5-6	AO3 4.5.2
	Level 2: an evaluation is given with mostly relevant detail, which demonstrates a reasonable understanding of the relevant principles. The evaluation may not be completely logical and may be missing some detail.		3-4	
	Level 1: discrete relevant points are made which demonstrate some understanding of the relevant principles.		1-2	
	No relevant content		0	

Question	Answer(s)	Extra info	Mark(s)	AO/Spec ref.
	Indicative content **Method** • only recording the shortest time for each student is not as representative as taking the mean result for each student • only using the right hand means that some students may not be using their dominant hand • different numbers of girls and boys is taken into account by taking mean results • sample sizes are small **Conclusion** • it is correct that the mean time for the girls is less than for the boys • the results for the boys show more variation than for the girls • if the longest boys' result (0.32) is discounted then boys overall have the shortest reaction time • the conclusion is based on a small sample size • the conclusion should only apply to this way of measuring reaction time			
08.2	receptor = ear effector = hand muscles		1 1	AO2 4.5.2
08.3	electric impulses along neurones/nerve cells		1 1	AO1 4.5.2
08.4	no – no mark pressing the button is a conscious action **or** pressing the button is not an automatic action		 1	AO2 4.5.2

Set A – Chemistry: Paper 3

Question	Answer(s)	Mark(s)	AO/Spec ref.
01.1	O_2	1	AO2 5.1.1.1
01.2	all atoms have an equal number of protons and electrons	1	AO1 5.1.1.4
01.3		1	AO1 5.1.1.7
01.4	add water, filter, heat and cool to crystallise	1	AO1 5.1.1.2
01.5	$Ca(HCO_3)_2$ has two carbon atoms	1	AO1 5.1.1.1
01.6	Ca (calcium)	1	AO1 5.2.1.2
01.7	it has 11 protons it has 11 electrons it has 12 neutrons	1 1 1	AO1 5.1.1.5

Question	Answer(s)	Mark(s)	AO/Spec ref.
02.1	no regular order	1	AO1
	all particles very close together / touching	1	5.2.2.1
	allow a partially filled box with all the liquid arranged like the above but collected in the bottom, as if the box were a container.		
02.2	at 1500 °C, silver chloride is a liquid	1	AO2
			5.2.2.1
	oxygen has the lowest melting point	1	
02.3	silver chloride	1	AO2
	sodium chloride	1	5.2.2.3
03.1	Exothermic	1	AO1
			5.5.1.1
03.2	Endothermic	1	AO1
			5.5.1.2
03.3	any two from:	2	AO1
	thermal decomposition of metal carbonates (e.g. limestone to make cement)		5.5.1.1
	photosynthesis		
	making cool packs		
03.4	magnesium first and copper last	1	AO2
	aluminium after magnesium and before iron	1	5.4.1.2
	the most reactive metal will have the highest temperature difference / most energy given out	1	
03.5	Level 3: a coherent method is described with relevant detail, which demonstrates a broad understanding of the relevant scientific techniques, procedures and safety precautions. The steps in the method are logically ordered with the dependent and control variables correctly identified. The method would lead to the production of valid results. Students should justify their choice of equipment with reference to precision or accuracy. For example they should state that without insulation heat would be lost and this will result in inaccurate temperature readings.	5-6	AO2 5.4.1.2 5.5.1.1

Question	Answer(s)	Mark(s)	AO/Spec ref.
	Level 2: the bulk of a method is described with mostly relevant detail, which demonstrates a reasonable understanding of the relevant scientific techniques, procedures and safety precautions. The method may not be in a completely logical sequence and may be missing some detail. For example, students may not link the need for insulation with the accuracy of the temperature readings. They may mention repeat readings without justification for why this is important.	3-4	
	Level 1: simple statements are made which demonstrate some understanding of some of the relevant scientific techniques, procedures and safety precautions. The response may lack a logical structure and would not lead to the production of valid results.	1-2	
	No relevant content	0	

Indicative content
- Wear safety glasses, protective clothing and gloves when handling acids

Method
- record initial temperature of HCl with thermometer
- place HCl and metal in beaker
- allow time for reaction to complete / no more bubbles
- record final temperature with thermometer
- calculate temperature difference

Fair test
- same mass of metal
- same surface area of metal
- same volume and concentration of HCl
- same materials for reaction beaker

Reliable and precise data
- polystyrene reaction beaker
- insulate reaction vessel to prevent heat loss
- weighing scales to 2 d.p. to measure mass of metal
- metal surface cleaned with sand paper to remove oxide layer
- repeat experiments at least three times for reliability and calculate mean temperature difference
- use digital thermometer instead of alcohol thermometer if possible

Question	Answer(s)	Mark(s)	AO/Spec ref.
04.1	copper sulfate	1	AO1 5.4.2.2
04.2	excess copper oxide is left undissolved at the base of the vessel	1	AO1 5.4.2.3
04.3	$CaCO_3(s) + 2HCl(aq) \rightarrow CaCl_2(aq) + H_2O(l) + CO_2(g)$	1	AO1 5.1.1.1

Question	Answer(s)	Mark(s)	AO/Spec ref.
04.4	the mass will appear to decrease	1	AO1 5.3.1.3 5.2.2.2
04.5	correct plotting of points (at least four of five correct for mark)	1	AO2 AO3 5.4.2.2
	anomalous results circled (at 30 g)	1	
	line of best fit drawn (omitting anomalous results)	1	
04.6	44 g allow error carried forward (ecf) from graph allow 42–45 g	1	AO3 5.4.2.2
	as the amount of calcium carbonate increases, the amount of calcium chloride formed increases	1	
04.7	136.5 g	1	AO1
	total mass of the reactants and total mass of the products are always equal / law of conservation of mass	1	AO2 5.3.1.1
04.8	20 ÷ 4 needs to be dissolved in 250 cm³ of solution	1	AO2 5.3.2.5
	5 g	1	
04.9	calcium nitrate	1	AO2
	$Ca(NO_3)_2$	1	5.4.2.2
05.1	**Level 3:** a detailed and coherent comparison is given, which demonstrates a broad knowledge and understanding of the key scientific ideas. The response makes logical links between the points raised and uses sufficient examples to support these links. The choice of extraction process should be clearly linked to reactivity of the metal. For example sodium is extracted by electrolysis because it is more reactive than carbon and therefore cannot undergo displacement with carbon.	5-6	AO3 5.4.1.3
	Level 2: a description is given which demonstrates a reasonable knowledge and understanding of the key scientific ideas. Comparisons are made but may not be fully articulated and / or precise. Students may not refer specifically to the term "reduction", but may describe how iron ore is reacted with carbon to make iron.	3-4	

Question	Answer(s)	Mark(s)	AO/Spec ref.
	Level 1: simple statements are made which demonstrate a basic knowledge of some of the relevant ideas. The response may fail to make comparisons between the points raised.	1-2	
	No relevant content	0	
	Indicative content		
	Gold • occurs as a native element • very unreactive / chemically uncombined • no processes needed • very rare — not much gold present **Iron** • iron ore is very abundant • iron oxide is reduced with carbon • iron is less reactive than carbon • reduction is the removal of oxygen • occurs in the blast furnace at high temperatures • iron oxide + carbon → iron + carbon dioxide **Sodium** • sodium is more reactive than carbon so cannot be extracted by reduction • molten sodium chloride is electrolysed • graphite electrodes / lots of electricity • lots of energy is needed to melt the ore • sodium chloride is very abundant		
06.1		1	AO1 5.2.2
06.2	all electrons correctly shown on the reactant side	1	AO2 5.2.1.2
	all electrons correctly shown on the product side	1	
06.3		1	AO1 5.2.3
06.4	simple covalent form molecules / giant covalent form macromolecules	1	AO3 5.2.2.4 5.2.2.6
	weak intermolecular forces between simple molecules / none in giant covalent	1	
	simple covalent have low melting and boiling points / giant covalent molecules have high melting and boiling points	1	
07.1	iodine	1	AO1 5.1.2.6

Question	Answer(s)	Mark(s)	AO/Spec ref.
07.2	one pair of electrons shared	1	AO1
	three pairs of electrons remaining on outer shell of each atom	1	5.2.1.4
07.3	**Group 1** any two from: group 1 elements react more vigorously / violently / explosively as you go down the group more fizzing / bubbles as you go down the group example of a reaction (e.g lithium does not burst into flame, but potassium will spontaneously burst into flame with water) **Group 7** any two from the following: group 7 element higher up the group will displace the halogen in the salt lower down the group example of a reaction (e.g. chlorine will react with potassium iodide to produce grey iodine)	2 2	AO1 5.1.2.5; AO1 5.1.2.6.
08.1	iodine is formed at the anode	1	AO2 5.4.3.2
08.2	any two from: they are more reactive than carbon / cannot be extracted by reduction with carbon as they are too reactive it is too expensive to extract them by displacement with a more reactive metal they combine strongly with anions in their mineral ores	2	AO2 5.4.1.3
08.3	**cathode** any two from: copper ions and hydrogen ions would be attracted copper is less reactive than hydrogen copper metal is formed / brown coating of copper observed **anode** any two from: chloride and hydroxide ions are attracted chlorine is formed / distinctive smell / bleaches litmus paper bubbles of chlorine gas observed	2 2	AO2 5.4.3.4

Set A – Chemistry: Paper 4

Question	Answer(s)	Mark(s)	AO/Spec ref.
01.1	a glowing splint relights when held in the gas	1	AO1 5.8.2
01.2	carbon dioxide	1	AO1 5.9.1.2

Question	Answer(s)		Mark(s)	AO/Spec ref.
01.3	nitrogen		1	AO1
	oxygen		1	5.9.1.1
01.4	(in order)			AO1
	oxygen		1	5.9.1.2
	decreased		1	
	dissolved		1	
	carbonates		1	
01.5	distilled water is a pure substance as nothing has been added to it		2	AO1 5.8.1.1
	a pure substance has a fixed melting and boiling point			
01.6	cough mixture		1	AO1
	cleaning agent		1	5.8.1.2
02.1	A = global warming (climate change)		1	AO1 5.9.3.1
	B = acid rain		1	5.9.3.2
	C = particulates (carbon)		1	
	D = burning fossil fuels		1	
03.1	liquefied petroleum gas = 20–30 °C kerosene = 150–230 °C heavy fuel oil = above 370 °C	2 marks for all 3 correct; 1 mark for 1 correct	2	AO2 5.7.1.3
03.2	they are mixtures/ they are not pure		1	AO2 5.8.1.1
	mixtures do not have a fixed boiling point/ only pure substances have a fixed boiling point		1	
03.3	**Level 3:** a detailed and coherent explanation is given, which demonstrates a broad knowledge and understanding of the key scientific ideas. The response makes logical links between the points raised and uses sufficient examples to support these links. For example, students state that the greater the size of the molecule, the higher the boiling point and link this to the point of condensation within the respective position or temperature of the column.		5-6	AO1 AO2 5.7.1.2 5.7.1.3
	Level 2: an explanation is given which demonstrates a reasonable knowledge and understanding of the key scientific ideas. Comparisons are made but may not be fully articulated and/or precise. For example, students state that the greater the size of the molecule, the higher the boiling point but do not necessarily link this to the position of condensation within the column		3-4	

Question	Answer(s)		Mark(s)	AO/Spec ref.
	Level 1: simple statements are made which demonstrate a basic knowledge of some of the relevant ideas. The response may fail to make comparisons between the points raised.		1-2	
	No relevant content		0	
	Indicative content • crude oil is a mixture of hydrocarbons • the crude oil enters the fractionating column at the bottom • it is heated to a temperature above the boiling point of the fractions present (over 370 °C) • the mixtures/ fractions of hydrocarbons evaporate • the fractions/ mixtures of hydrocarbons have different length of C chains • the smallest chains have the lowest boiling points/ the largest chains have the highest boiling points • as the fractions/hydrocarbons rise up the column, the temperature decreases • the fractions/ mixtures cool as they go up and condense at the point in the column which is at a temperature equal to the boiling point range • the fractions cool and condense at their boiling point and are collected as liquids			
04.1			1	AO1 5.7.1.1
04.2	oxygen carbon dioxide allow correct symbols in place of words		1 1	AO2 5.7.1.3
04.3	it will be harder to combust/ it is less flammable		1	AO2 5.7.1.3
04.4	$C_{18}H_{38} \rightarrow 6C_2H_4 + C_6H_{14}$		1	AO1 5.1.1.1
04.5	add bromine water alkene will decolourise bromine water alkane will not decolourise / remain orange solution		1 1 1	AO1 5.7.1.4
05.1	natural materials: cotton, wool synthetic materials: plastics, nylon, pvc, polyester	3 marks for all six in correct column; 2 marks for 4 or 5 correct; 1 mark for 2 or 3; no marks for only one correct	3	AO1 5.10.1.1

Question	Answer(s)		Mark(s)	AO/Spec ref.
05.2	plastic production has gone up over time		1	AO3 5.10.1.1
	the rate of plastic production is increasing faster in more recent years		1	
05.3	the trend is likely to decrease any answer from: we are running out of crude oil plastics take a long time to degrade and cause waste storage problems new materials may be made from renewable sources and so are more biodegradable		1 1	AO3 5.10.1.1
05.4	corn starch is renewable whereas crude oil is a finite resource		1	AO1 5.10.1.1
06.1	use of limited (finite) natural resources/ named resource, e.g. limestone		1	AO2/ AO3 5.10.2.2
	use of energy/ fossil fuels in extracting new material		1	
	environmental impact, e.g. global climate change from CO_2 emissions/ eyesore from mining and quarrying/ reduced waste to landfill		1	
06.2	one advantage of glass one advantage of brick one disadvantage of glass one disadvantage of brick **advantages of glass from:** can be recycled easily to make new glass; plastic cannot sand and limestone are more abundant than crude oil less environmental impact in obtaining raw materials for glass making compared to obtaining crude oil, e.g. oil spills, glass is stronger/ harder/ less easily scratched than plastic **advantages of brick from:** less CO_2 is produced from the manufacture of brick as limestone is not decomposed as in the manufacture of concrete more raw materials needed to make concrete so more energy used compared to brick more impact on landscape to obtain raw materials for concrete as more are needed **disadvantages of glass from:** more energy required to make glass compared to plastics plastics are longer lasting/ do not break as easily as glass **disadvantages of brick from:** concrete can be made into different shapes for buildings/ more versatile easier to make new concrete from old concrete compared to new bricks from old		1 1 1 1	AO3 5.10.2.2

Question	Answer(s)	Mark(s)	AO/Spec ref.
07.1	potable water contains low levels of dissolved salts, pure water has no dissolved salts	1	AO1 5.10.1.2 5.8.1.1
	potable water contains low levels of microbes, pure water has no microbes	1	
07.2	none of the sterilising agents remove all the pathogens	1	AO3 5.10.1.2
	any comparative statement with the use of data (e.g. ozone removes 90% of pathogens, whereas chlorine removes less)	1	
07.3	any two from	2	AO3 5.10.1.2
	same amount of pathogens to start with		
	sterilising agent exposed to pathogens for the same length of time		
	same volume and type of water		
07.4	any four from:	4	AO2 5.10.1.3
	sewage requires sedimentation to produce sewage sludge and effluent		
	sewage sludge needs to be anaerobically digested		
	effluent from sewage sedimentation is treated with aerobic biological treatment		
	sewage treatment takes longer than ground water treatment		
	sewage treatment is more costly		
	sewage sludge may be used and sold as fertiliser		
	sewage sludge may be used to produce methane as a fuel		
08.1	top curve = powder; lower curve = ribbon	1	AO2 AO3 5.6.1.1 5.6.1.2
	appropriate lines of best fit	1	
	omission of anomalous result at 120 s on lower line	1	
08.2	rate = 40 ÷ 120	1	AO2 5.6.1.1
	= 0.333	1	
	cm^3/s	1	
08.3	powder has a greater surface area	1	AO2 5.6.1.3
	more frequent collisions between acid particles and the solid	1	
08.4	particles have higher energy, therefore…	1	AO2 5.6.1.3
	…more frequent collisions	1	
	…more successful/effective collisions	1	

Set A – Physics: Paper 5

Question	Answer(s)	Extra info	Mark(s)	AO/Spec ref.
01.1	small, well separated circles drawn randomly in the box		1	AO1 6.3.1.1
01.2	moving around constantly randomly / in all directions		1 1	AO1 6.3.3.1
01.3	internal energy		1	AO1 6.3.2.1
01.4	increasing the temperature increases the speed of the gas particles	no more than two boxes ticked	1	AO1 6.3.3.1 6.3.2.1
	increasing the temperature increases the gas pressure		1	
02.1	the resistors are connected in series	only one box ticked	1	AO1 6.2.2
02.2	($R_{total} = R_1 + R_2 = 5 + 5$) total resistance = 10 (Ω)		1	AO2 6.2.2
02.3	current $\frac{1.5}{10}$ current = 0.15 (A)	1 mark for substitution 1 mark for answer correct answer with no working shown = 2 marks	2	AO2 6.2.2 6.2.1.3
02.4	ammeter reading decreases voltmeter reading doesn't change	1 mark each only two boxes ticked	2	AO2 6.2.2
03.1	protons: 53		1	AO1 6.4.1.2
	neutrons: 74		1	
	electrons: 53		1	
03.2	nucleus (is unstable and) emits radiation		1	AO1 6.4.2.1
	to become more stable		1	
03.3	(high speed) electron is ejected from the nucleus		1	AO1 6.4.2.1
	as a neutron turns into a proton		1	
03.4	**Level 2:** coherent and detailed method to enable a valid value for the half-life to be obtained		3–4	AO2 6.4.2.1 6.4.2.3
	Level 1: some relevant content but may not produce a valid half-life value		1–2	

Question	Answer(s)	Extra info	Mark(s)	AO/Spec ref.
	No relevant content		0	
	Indicative content • record the (initial) reading of activity (or count rate) and start a stopclock / stopwatch • take activity (or count rate) readings as time passes • plot a graph of activity (or count rate) against time • use the graph to find the time for the activity (or count rate) to fall to half its (initial) value • obtain a 2nd half-life value from a different section of the graph • calculate an average of the two values	consideration of background count not required		
04.1	volume (= 5.0 × 2.0 × 2.0) = 20 (cm³)	accept correct answer with no working shown	1	AO2 6.3.1.1
04.2	$density = \dfrac{mass}{volume}$		1	AO1 6.3.1.1
04.3	$density = \dfrac{144}{20}$ density = 7.2 (g/cm³)	1 mark for substitution 1 mark for answer correct answer with no working shown = 2 marks	2	AO2 6.3.1.1
04.4	both the density of tin and zinc are (very) close to the calculated density value for the metal block the student's (length, width and height / volume) data has too few significant figures / not measured precisely enough to decide between zinc and tin	1 mark for either statement allow alternative suggestion consistent with error carried forward from 04.3	1	AO3 6.3.1.1

Question	Answer(s)	Extra info	Mark(s)	AO/Spec ref.
05.1	independent variable: length		1	AO3 6.2.1.3
	dependent variable: resistance		1	
	control variable: thickness/ material (of wire)		1	
05.2	**Level 2:** a detailed and coherent plan covering all the major steps is provided. The steps are presented in a logical order that could be followed by another person to obtain valid results.		3–4	AO2 6.2.1.3
	Level 1: simple statements relating to relevant apparatus or steps are made but may not follow a logical sequence. The plan would not enable another person to obtain valid results.		1–2	
	No relevant content		0	
	Indicative content • the length of wire between the crocodile clips is measured with a meter rule • the switch is closed • the reading on the ammeter is recorded • the reading on the voltmeter is recorded • the voltmeter reading is divided by the ammeter reading to determine the wire's resistance • switch opened to stop wire overheating • the measurements are repeated for different lengths of wire • plot a graph of resistance against length			
05.3	random error	only one box ticked	1	AO3 6.2.1.3
05.4	straight line drawn, positive gradient, through the origin		1	AO1 6.2.1.3 6.2.1.4
06.1	energy needed to raise the temperature of 1 kg of a material by 1°C		1	AO1 6.1.1.3
06.2	it decreased	only one box ticked	1	AO1 6.1.1.1
06.3	ΔE = 0.1 × 4200 × 10 increase in thermal energy of water = 4200 (J)	1 mark for substitution 1 mark for answer correct answer with no working shown = 2 marks	2	AO2 6.1.1.3

Question	Answer(s)	Extra info	Mark(s)	AO/Spec ref.
06.4	specific heat capacity = $\dfrac{4200}{(0.1 \times 70)}$ specific heat capacity = 600 (J/ kg °C)	1 mark for substitution (allow error carried forward from 06.3) 1 mark for answer correct answer with no working shown = 2 marks	2	AO2 6.1.1.3
06.5	to the beaker / surroundings		1	AO1 6.1.2.1
06.6	any one from: insulate the beaker use a polystyrene cup instead of the glass beaker put a lid on the beaker	any one suggestion for 1 mark	1	AO3 6.1.2.1
07.1	uranium	only one box ticked	1	AO1 6.1.3
07.2	**Level 3:** coherent and detailed account with several comparisons of reliability and environmental effects and including both similarities and differences		5–6	AO3 6.1.3
	Level 2: clear account with some valid comparisons of reliability and environmental effect		3–4	
	Level 1: some relevant comments regarding reliability and environmental effects but comparisons may not be made. The descriptions are vague and lack sufficient detail		1–2	
	No relevant content		0	

Question	Answer(s)	Extra info	Mark(s)	AO/Spec ref.
	Indicative content **Wind power:** • renewable / doesn't run out • not reliable / predictable: only supplies energy when it is windy • usually windy somewhere in the UK • does not cause (atmospheric) pollution • no greenhouse gas emissions/does not contribute as much to climate change • noise disturbance may be an issue • possible hazard to birds • turbines may be considered to have a negative visual impact **Coal power:** • not renewable • reliable (always available, able to generate continuously) • not dependent on the weather • significant coal reserves worldwide • creates atmospheric pollution • produces greenhouse gas emissions • which contributes to climate change / global warming • environmental pollution, loss of habitat in areas where coal is mined • mining can be dangerous			
08.1	gravitational potential energy = mass × gravitational field strength × height	accept $E_{(p)} = mgh$	1	AO1 6.1.1.2
08.2	$E_p = 50 \times 9.8 \times 10$ increase in gravitational potential energy store 4900 J	1 mark for substitution 1 mark for answer correct answer with no working shown = 2 marks	2	AO2 6.1.1.2
08.3	gravitational potential energy to kinetic energy	only one box ticked	1	AO1 6.1.1.1
08.4	kinetic energy = 0.5 × mass × (velocity)²	accept $E_{(k)} = \frac{1}{2}mv^2$	1	AO1 6.1.1.2
08.5	$E_k = \frac{1}{2} \times 50 \times 6^2$ store of kinetic energy 900 J	1 mark for substitution 1 mark for evaluation correct answer with no working 2 marks	2	AO2 6.1.1.2
08.6	apply oil / lubricant (to the axle)		1	AO1 6.1.2.1
09.1	time taken = 220 – 20 = 200 (s)	1 mark for values from graph 1 mark for answer correct answer with no working shown = 2 marks	2	AO3 6.3.2.3

Question	Answer(s)	Extra info	Mark(s)	AO/Spec ref.
09.2	three of: particles become (slightly) further apart arrangement of particles becomes less ordered particles can move around, passing each other particles change from vibrating (about a fixed position) to moving around passing each other speed of vibration/kinetic enery of particles increases as solid heats up, till melting point speed/kinetic energy of particles remains same while oil is changing state from solid to liquid (at melting point)	1 mark for any statement maximum 3 marks	3	AO1 6.3.1.1
09.3	energy transferred = power × time	1 mark accept power = energy transfered/ time	1	AO1 6.2.4.2
09.4	energy transferred = 100 × 200 energy transferred = 20 000 (J)	1 mark for substitution 1 mark for answer correct answer with no working shown = 2 marks	2	AO2 6.2.4.2
09.5	(thermal energy for a change of state = mass × specific latent heat) $20\,000 = 0.080 × L$ $L = \frac{20\,000}{0.080}$ specific latent heat = 250 000 J/kg	1 mark for substitution into correct equation 1 mark for evaluation correct answer with no working = 2 marks	2	AO2 6.3.2.3

Set A – Physics: Paper 6

Question	Answer(s)	Extra info	Mark(s)	AO/Spec ref.
01.1	any one from: air resistance / water resistance / drag friction tension normal contact force	1 mark for any correct example	1	AO1 6.5.1.2
01.2	any one from: gravity / weight magnetic force / magnetism	1 mark for any correct example	1	AO1 6.5.1.2
01.3	tension / the force on the string gravity (accept weight)	1 mark 1 mark no other forces listed	2	AO1 6.5.1.2
01.4	work done = 4.0 × 0.25 = 1.0 (N m)	1 mark for substitution 1 mark for answer correct answer with no working shown = 2 marks	2	AO2 6.5.2
02.1	the north pole of one magnet exerts **an attractive force** on the south pole of a second magnet		1	AO1 6.7.1.1
	the north pole of a magnet exerts **an attractive force** on a piece of magnetic material such as iron		1	
	the north pole of one magnet exerts **a repulsive force** on the north pole of a second magnet		1	
	the south pole of one magnet exerts **a repulsive force** on the south pole of a second magnet		1	
02.2	a permanent magnet creates its own magnetic field		1	AO1 6.7.1.1
	an induced magnet becomes a magnet only when it is placed in a magnetic field (e.g. of a permanent magnet)		1	
	and loses its magnetism when removed from the magnetic field		1	
02.3		1 mark for one arrow on each line pointing from N to S	2	AO1 6.7.1.2
02.4	**Level 2:** a clear, detailed plan covering all steps presented in a logical order. The plan could be followed by another person to complete the task as required		3–4	AO2 6.7.1.2

Question	Answer(s)	Extra info	Mark(s)	AO/Spec ref.
	Level 1: some relevant statements but the plan could not be followed by another person to complete the task		1–2	
	No relevant content		0	
	Indicative content: • place the bar magnet on a piece of paper and draw around the magnet • place the compass close to (one end of) the magnet • use a pencil to mark a dot at the point that the needle (of the compass) is pointing • move the compass so that its centre is over the dot just made • mark another dot at the point that the needle (of the compass) is now pointing • remove the compass and join the dots with an arrow from the first dot to the 2nd dot • keep repeating the process until the arrows form a complete line from one point on the magnet to another allow any of the above points conveyed in a clear diagram			
03.1	the resultant force on a stationary object is zero the resultant force on an object moving at a steady speed is zero	1 mark 1 mark no more than two boxed ticked	2	AO1 6.5.4.2.1
03.2	E	1 mark only one box ticked	1	AO1 6.5.1.2
03.3	F G	1 mark for each correct letter no more than two boxes ticked	2	AO1 6.5.1.2
03.4	B	1 mark only one box ticked	1	AO1 6.5.1.3
03.5	A	1 mark only one box ticked	1	AO1 6.5.1.2
03.6	acceleration = $\dfrac{14-10}{2.5}$ acceleration = 1.6 unit: m/s^2	1 mark for substitution 1 mark for answer correct answer with no working shown = 2 marks 1 mark for unit	2 1	AO2 6.5.4.1.5 AO1 6.5.4.1.5
03.7	Resultant force = 4000 × 1.6 Resultant force = 6400 (N)	1 mark for substitution 1 mark for evaluation correct answer with no working shown = 2 marks allow error carried forward from 03.6	2	AO2 6.5.4.2.2
04.1	number of waves / vibrations (produced / passing a point) each second	allow number of times it moves up and down again	1	AO2 6.6.1.2
04.2	5.0 Hz	only one box ticked	1	AO2 6.6.1.2
04.3	wavelength		1	AO1 6.6.1.2
04.4	transverse	only one box ticked	1	AO1 6.6.1.1
04.5	put a floating object in the tank observe the object just move up and down, not across the tank, as the wave passes		1 1	AO2 6.6.1.1
04.6	wave speed = frequency × wavelength	accept $v = f\lambda$	1	AO1 6.6.1.2
04.7	wave speed = 3.0 × 4.0 wave speed = 12 (cm/s)	1 mark for substitution 1 mark for answer correct answer with no working shown = 2 marks	1 1	AO2 6.6.1.2
04.8	independent variable: depth dependent variable: speed		1 1	AO3 6.6.1.2
04.9	wave speed is greater in deeper water at greater depths, the rate at which speed increases with depth is reduced	1 mark 1 mark allow any other correct conclusion	2	AO3 6.6.1.2
05.1	any one from: force, displacement, velocity, acceleration	1 mark for one correct quantity	1	AO1 6.5.4.1.1

Question	Answer(s)	Extra info	Mark(s)	AO/Spec ref.
05.2	any two from: at first the car speeds up / accelerates in the middle of the journey, the car moves with a steady speed near the end of the journey the car slows down/decelerates the car stops at the end of the journey	1 mark for any correct statement maximum 2 marks	2	AO3 6.5.4.1.4
05.3	60 (m)		1	AO2 6.5.4.1.4
05.4	distance (travelled) = speed × time	accept speed = distance travelled/time	1	AO1 6.5.4.1.2
05.5	$60 = v \times 4$ $v = \dfrac{60}{4}$ average speed = 15 m/s	1 mark for substitution and rearranging 1 mark for answer correct answer with no working shown = 2 marks allow error carried forward from 05.3	1 1	AO2 6.5.4.1.2
06.1	the temperature of the hot water could affect the amount of infrared emitted (from the container's surface)	Do not accept 'to keep it a fair test' without further detail	1	AO3 6.6.2.1
06.2	the amount (or intensity) of infrared detected (by the sensor) could depend on its distance from the surface	Do not accept 'to keep it a fair test' without further detail	1	AO3 6.6.2.1

Question	Answer(s)	Extra info	Mark(s)	AO/Spec ref.
06.3	any two from: the amount (or intensity) of infrared emitted (per second per square cm) depends on the surface black surfaces emit more infrared (per second per square cm) than aluminium surfaces for the same colour, a dull surface emits more infrared (per second per square cm) than a shiny surface	1 mark each for any two correct conclusions	2	AO3 6.6.2.1
06.4	have four sensors and take the readings for all four surfaces at the same time take a reading for one surface at a particular temperature, then repeat for each surface at that temperature (refilling the container with boiling water and checking temperature each time)	1 mark for either suggestion or other sensible suggestion	1	AO3 6.6.2.1
07.1	Level 3: a coherent plan covering all steps presented in a logical order. The plan could be followed by another person to obtain valid results. Procedures ensure errors are minimised		5–6	AO2 6.5.3
	Level 2: a clear plan covering the major steps presented in a logical order. The plan could be followed by another person to obtain valid results		3–4	

Question	Answer(s)	Extra info	Mark(s)	AO/Spec ref.
	Level 1: some relevant statements but the plan could not be followed by another person to obtain valid results		1–2	
	No relevant content		0	

	Indicative content:
	• with no weight attached, the metre rule reading in line with the pointer is recorded.
	• a standard/known weight is attached to the spring
	• the length of the stretched spring is indicated by the pointer attached to the bottom of the spring
	• pointer ensures length measurement made systematically (consistently)
	• the length of the stretched spring is measured using the metre rule
	• extension is found by subtracting the unstretched length from the stretched length
	• repeat the procedure with different weights to minimise errors:
	  – view the pointer from the same horizontal level
	  – take repeat readings and average
	• analysis: plot a graph of extension versus stretching force			

07.2	C		1	AO3 6.5.3
07.3	C		1	AO3 6.5.3
07.4	A		1	AO3 6.5.3
07.5	B		1	AO2 6.5.3
07.6	force (applied to a spring) = spring constant × extension	accept $F = k\,e$	1	AO1 6.5.3
07.7	extension = 0.335 – 0.085 = 0.25 (m) $8.0 = k \times 0.25$ $k = \dfrac{8.0}{0.25}$ spring constant = 32 (N/m)	1 mark for correct extension 1 mark for substitution and rearranging 1 mark for answer correct answer with no working shown = 3 marks	3	AO2 6.5.3

262 Combined Science Set A - Answers

©HarperCollins*Publishers* 2019

Set B – Biology: Paper 1

Question	Answer(s)	Extra info	Mark(s)	AO/Spec ref.
01.1	any one from: skin, mucus lining of respiratory tract, any other suitable answer		1	AO1 4.3.1.6
01.2	antibody production		1	AO1 4.3.1.6
01.3			1	AO1 4.2.2.3
01.4	kill bacteria inside the body		1	AO1 4.3.1.8
	specific bacteria are killed by specific antibiotics		1	
01.5	painkillers treat the symptoms of disease		1	AO1 4.3.1.8
	but do not kill pathogens/ antibiotics kill bacteria		1	
01.6	virus		1	AO1 4.3.1.2
01.7	distinctive 'mosaic' pattern of discolouration on the leaves		1	AO1 4.3.1.2
01.8	black spot		1	AO1 4.3.1.4
02.1	enzymes		1	AO1 4.2.2.1
02.2	amino acids	accept fats (instead of lipids)	1	AO1 4.2.2.1
	lipids		1	4.4.2.3
02.3	**either of:** • buffer must be added to the enzyme before the starch is added – as the reaction will start as soon as the enzyme and starch meet • if no buffer (or added afterwards) results will not be valid as the pH will be changed after the reaction has started		1	AO2 4.2.2.1
02.4	a control makes it easier to compare colours		1	AO2 4.2.2.1
	as the water in the control doesn't contain any starch/so you can be sure all the starch is gone/digested/broken down, if it is the same colour as the control		1	
02.5	85 + 80 + 75 = 240	must state unit (seconds) for third mark	2	AO1 4.2.2.1
	240/3 = 80			
	seconds		1	
02.6	pH 7		1	AO2 4.2.2.1

Question	Answer(s)	Extra info	Mark(s)	AO/Spec ref.
03.1	animal cells, line drawn from: • plasma membrane only, no cell wall • carbohydrate stored as glycogen plant cells, line drawn from: • chloroplasts • large vacuole		3	AO1 4.1.1.2
03.2	to keep the specimen flat		1	AO1 4.1.1.2
03.3	iodine solution		1	AO1 4.1.1.2
03.4	Meristem / area of cell division	1 mark for drawing, with distinct meristem area 1 mark for label	2	AO2 4.2.3.1 4.1.1.2
	scale bar should be approximately 10 mm long and labelled 2mm	1 mark for sensible units/scale (1 cm long scale. Units mm and μm) 1 mark for correct scale bar	2	
04.1	active = 3000 incidences (allow ± 1000)	1 mark for both readings	1	AO3 4.2.2.5 4.2.2.6
	drink less alcohol = 12 000 incidences (allow ± 1000) and therefore drinking less alcohol is about 4 times more effective than being active, in preventing cancer	must include the comparison for second mark	1	
04.2	eat sufficient fruit and veg lots of fibre low salt low processed/red meat low alcohol	must include low alcohol for 2 marks (to reward recognising alcohol/ drinks are part of the diet) and at least two others	2	AO2 4.2.2.5 4.2.2.6
04.3	lung cancer	accept lung by itself	1	AO3 4.2.2.6

Question	Answer(s)	Extra info	Mark(s)	AO/Spec ref.
04.4	benign tumours any one from: growths of abnormal cells contained in one area usually within a membrane do not invade other parts of the body malignant tumour cells are cancers plus any one from: invade neighbouring tissues spread to different parts of the body spread in the blood form secondary tumours	must link malignant tumours to being cancers	1 2	AO1 4.2.2.7
05.1	white blood cells are producing antibodies in response to the presence of Lumpius/ pathogen/ vaccination	accept lymphocytes accept: detect antigens on dead/ inactive Lumpius	1	AO2 4.3.1.6 4.3.1.7
05.2	any two from: white blood cells instantly recognise live Lumpius/ pathogen (because it has the same antigens as the vaccine) and respond more quickly and in larger numbers to the infection by producing many specific antibodies, which lock onto the Lumpius/ pathogen and kill them before person becomes ill/ person is immune/ has immunity	accept lymphocytes must state 'more quickly' or equivalent	2	AO2 4.3.1.6 4.3.1.7
05.3	**because** many specific antibodies are produced, more quickly when volunteers are infected with live Lumpius/pathogen		2	AO3 4.3.1.7

Question	Answer(s)	Extra info	Mark(s)	AO/Spec ref.
05.4	any three from: preclinical trials in laboratory on cells, tissues and live animals clinical trials using healthy volunteers and patients tested for toxicity, efficacy and dose very low doses at start of the clinical trial if drug is safe, further clinical trials are carried out to find the optimum dose for the drug	must be in correct order	3	AO2 4.3.1.9
06.1	any two from: by moving the lamp/light source by measuring the distance, i.e. using convenience distance intervals by using a variable brightness lamp		2	AO2 4.4.1.2
06.2	count the number of bubbles over a given time period or specific time given, e.g. count bubbles for 1 min		1 1	AO2 4.4.1.2
06.3	**Level 3:** a detailed and coherent explanation is provided with most of the relevant content, which demonstrates a comprehensive understanding of the investigation and the order in which it is carried out. The response gives logical steps, with reasons		5–6	AO2 4.4.1.2
	Level 2: a detailed and coherent explanation is provided. The student has a broad understanding of the investigation. The response gives mainly logical steps with some reasoning		3–4	
	Level 1: simple descriptions of the investigation are made along with reference to photosynthesis. The response demonstrates limited logical linking of points		1–2	
	No relevant content		0	

Question	Answer(s)	Extra info	Mark(s)	AO/Spec ref.
	Indicative content • set up apparatus as in diagram • make sure plant is photosynthesising (can see bubbles of oxygen) • measure and record the temperature of water in beaker; the water is intended to maintain a constant temperature (buffer), so the temperature should be taken periodically and kept constant; controlling other variables • measure and place lamp a specified distance from apparatus – carry out at several different distances of lamp (five distances 10 cm apart) • allow plant to acclimatise to each new distance of the lamp/light intensity (2 mins) • record production rate of oxygen and repeat at least three times for each distance of the lamp/light intensity • calculate mean production oxygen rate			
06.4	lots of sunshine = lots of oxygen produced/ high rate of photosynthesis and therefore lots of oxygen = for fish respiration	allow converse lack of sunshine/in shady area = lower rate of photosynthesis/less oxygen produced allow converse in shade = not so good for fish	1 1	AO3 4.4.1.2
07.1	chloroplast		1	AO2 4.1.1.2
07.2	**Level 3:** a detailed and coherent description is provided with most of the relevant content, which demonstrates a comprehensive understanding of photosynthesis. The response is logical		5–6	AO1 4.4.1.1 4.4.1.2 4.4.1.3
	Level 2: a detailed and coherent description is provided. The student has a broad understanding of photosynthesis. The response makes mainly logical steps with some linkage		3–4	
	Level 1: simple descriptions of photosynthesis are made. The response demonstrates limited logical linking of points		1–2	
	No relevant content		0	

Question	Answer(s)	Extra info	Mark(s)	AO/Spec ref.

	Indicative content
	 describe photosynthesis:
	 • carbon dioxide +water light glucose +oxygen
	 • endothermic reaction
	 • energy is transferred from the environment
	 • to the chloroplasts by light
	 the factors that affect it:
	 • rate of photosynthesis affected by:
	   o temperature
	   o light intensity
	   o carbon dioxide concentration
	 • amount of chlorophyll
	 and how plants use the products:
	 • glucose produced converted to starch, fats and oils for storage
	 • used for respiration
	 • used to produce cellulose, which strengthens the cell wall
	 • used to produce amino acids for protein synthesis
		accept CO_2, H_2O, O_2 and $C_6H_{12}O_6$		

08.1	accept answers in order of 25 cm²	second mark for correct units	2	AO3 4.1.3.1
08.2	$(228/25) \times 100 = 912\%$ allow error carried forward from 08.1	3 marks for calculation (ecf)	3	AO3 4.1.3.1
08.3	Fennec foxes have larger ears so there is a larger surface area to lose heat from	allow converse (Arctic foxes have small ears (small surface area) to conserve heat) for 1 mark	2	AO3 4.1.3.1

Set B – Biology: Paper 2

Question	Answer(s)	Extra info	Mark(s)	AO/Spec ref.
01.1	abiotic		1	AO 1 4.7.1.1
01.2	any two from: light space water mineral ions	do not accept food	2	AO 1 4.7.1.1
01.3	any two from: food territory water	do not accept space	2	AO 1 4.7.1.1
01.4	interdependence		1	AO 1 4.7.1.1
01.5	a community in which all the species and environmental factors are in balance		1	AO 1 4.7.1.1
	so that population sizes remain fairly constant		1	
01.6	carbon dioxide		2	AO1 4.7.2.2
	mineral ions			
02.1	**nervous system:** fast acting acts for short time acts in a specific area electrical **hormonal system:** slow acting acts for long time acts more generally chemical	for each mark, a line must be drawn from each of the opposing descriptions; i.e. for first mark one line drawn from fast acting to nervous system and one line drawn from slow acting to hormonal system (1 mark)	4	AO1 4.5.2 4.5.3.1
02.2	either: control of body temperature or control of water content		1	AO1 4.5.1
02.3	any one from: eye ear skin tongue		1	AO1 4.5.1
02.4	brain, spinal cord or pancreas		1	AO1 4.5.1
02.5	muscle or gland	accept specific example	1	AO1 4.5.1
02.6	85 + 87 + 83 + 81 = 336	must state units for third mark	1	AO3 4.5.2
	336/4 = 84		1	
	ms		1	

Question	Answer(s)	Extra info	Mark(s)	AO/Spec ref.
02.7	drinking alcohol slows down reactions times		1	AO1 4.5.2
03.1	sensible scales on correct axis		1	AO3 4.5.3.2
	correctly plotting points		1	
	drawing line – joining points or line of best fit		1	
	labels on axes – y axis = percentage of population who have Type 2 diabetes (%),and x axis = mean body mass (kg)		1	

Question	Answer(s)	Extra info	Mark(s)	AO/Spec ref.
03.2	correlation/positive correlation, as mean body mass increases so does percentage/incidence of type 2 diabetes		1	AO3 4.5.3.2
03.3	either: **oral** contraceptives that contain hormones to **inhibit FSH production** so that **no eggs mature** or **oral contraceptives/ Injection**/implant/ skin patch of slow release **progesterone/ oral contraceptive of oestrogen and progesterone** to maintain the uterus lining and so prevent the menstrual cycle, therefore **inhibiting the maturation/release of eggs**	must state two of three emboldened text (or equivalent) must relate to only **one** method (i.e. not a mix of methods)	2	AO1 4.5.3.4
04.1	zebrafish		1	AO3 4.6.4
04.2	fugu and green spotted puffer		1	AO3 4.6.4
04.3	167.7 million years ago	must give units accept mya	1	AO3 4.6.4
04.4	insufficient evidence currently to be more accurate		1	AO3 4.6.3.2 4.6.4
04.5	they are not able to interbreed		1	AO2 4.6.2.2
	to produce fertile offspring		1	

Question	Answer(s)	Extra info	Mark(s)	AO/Spec ref.
04.6	either: fossils or DNA profiling or antibiotic resistance (in case of bacteria)		1	AO1 4.6.2.1 4.6.3.2 4.6.3.4
05.1	pollen grain (nucleus)		1	AO1 4.6.1.1
05.2	mitosis		1	AO1 4.6.1.1
05.3	any two from: meiosis occurs copies of the genetic information are made the cell divides (twice) / four gametes are formed the resulting cells have half the number of chromosomes/amount of genetic material as the parent cell		2	AO1 4.6.1.2
05.4	heterozygous		1	AO2 4.6.1.4
05.5	mice A and B		1	AO2 4.6.1.4
05.6	brown		1	AO2 4.6.1.4
05.7	any three from: gamete would contain brown fur allele from Mouse B and white fur allele from Mouse C offspring would receive one of each/one brown fur allele and one white fur allele a dominant allele is always expressed, even if only one copy is present brown fur gene is dominant and therefore expressed/offspring have brown fur a recessive allele is only expressed if two copies are present (therefore no dominant allele present)		3	AO2 4.6.1.4
05.8	XY / they are different (to each other)		1	AO1 4.6.1.6
05.9	selective breeding		1	AO2 4.6.2.3
05.10	genetic engineering		1	AO2 4.6.2.4

Question	Answer(s)	Extra info	Mark(s)	AO/Spec ref.
05.11	the gardener's method: • is the traditional method of breeding together individuals with desired characteristics • is the more natural method • takes a long time (many generations) • offspring won't definitely have trait the gardener wants		1 (one point required)	AO2 4.6.2.3 4.6.2.4
	the farmer's method: • is more technical • is faster by transplanting specific genes for desired characteristics • offspring will definitely have the desired traits • is more expensive		1 (one point required)	
06.1	any one from: green plants algae/weed producers/primary producers		1	AO2 4.7.2.1 4.7.4.1
06.2	*T. sarasinorum* numbers increase and they eat lots of fish eggs		1	AO2 4.7.1.1
	therefore fewer fish survive from the eggs and there are fewer to eat, so 'elongated' eats more shrimp		1	4.7.2.1
	'thicklip' numbers decrease as they are now in direct competition for shrimp, not enough shrimp for all		1	
06.3	live in different habitats (1 mark only)		1	AO2 4.7.1.1
	T. opudi lives in bush cover and rocks, whereas *T. wahjui* lives on the muddy bottom		1	4.7.2.1
06.4	any two from: weed would die off/less weed cover *T. opudi* less opportunity to hide from predators/*T. opudi* more preyed upon *T. opudi* would not be able to adapt/evolve quickly enough to a different habitat food sources of *T. opudi* may become scarce/*T. opudi* would not be able to adapt/evolve quickly enough to eat a different food source competition from *T. wahjui* (not directly affected by weed disease)		2	AO2 4.6.3.3
06.5	any one from: sewage fertilizer run-off toxic chemicals any named example of toxic chemical		1	AO1 4.7.3.2

Question	Answer(s)	Extra info	Mark(s)	AO/Spec ref.
07.1	population size means the number of individuals of a species that live in a habitat (number)		1	AO1 4.7.1.1
	population density is the number of individuals in a given/specific area		1	
07.2	transect		1	AO2 4.7.1.1
07.3	systematic sampling:			AO2 4.7.1.1
	at regular intervals (e.g. every 50 cm)		1	
	intervals must be sufficient to capture the changes in vegetative cover		1	
07.4	construct further transects at 10 m intervals/ other sensible distance down the path		1	AO2 4.7.1.1
	take quadrats at the same distances as before (as suggested in 07.3) along these transects		1	
	calculate the means at each quadrat place along the length of the path (add up all the plantains and divide by number of quadrats along the length of the path) to give mean number across the path		1	
07.5	plants compete with each other for limited resources/many plants at verge, lots of competition		1	AO3 4.7.1
	plantain leaves are tough/have adapted to being trampled and may out complete more delicate plants, which are trampled in the middle of the path		1	4.7.1.3 4.7.1.4

Set B – Chemistry: Paper 3

Question	Answer(s)	Extra info	Mark(s)	AO/Spec ref.
01.1	the nucleus contains both protons and neutrons.		1	AO1 5.1.1.3
01.2	element — a substance that is made from only one type of atom		1	AO1 5.1.1.1 5.1.1.2
	compound — where two or more substances have chemically combined			
	mixture — where two or more substances are together but can be separated			
	all three correct for one mark			
01.3	Be and Ca		1	AO1 5.1.1.7
01.4	simple molecular		1	AO1 5.2.1.1
01.5	dull appearance		1	AO1 5.1.2.3
	low boiling point		1	

Question	Answer(s)	Extra info	Mark(s)	AO/Spec ref.
02.1	Z	in this order only	1	AO2 5.1.2.1
	C		1	
	X or Y		1	
	Z		1	
02.2	name of gas = hydrogen		1	AO1 5.8.2.1
	test = squeaky pop (when lit)		1	
02.3		one mark for full outer shell **and** square brackets	2	AO2 5.2.1.2
		one mark for correct charge +/1+/+1		
		can use dots or crosses to show electrons		
02.4	any three from (potassium):		3	AO1 5.1.2.5
	produces lilac flame			
	reacts faster / dissolves faster			
	bubbles / fizzes more			
	moves quicker / more			
	melts			
02.5	any three from:	allow converse arguments	3	AO2 5.1.2.5
	increasing size of atom / number of shells / atomic radius / more shells			
	increased shielding			
	outer electron / shell further from nucleus (must be talking about outer electrons)*			
	so less attraction for outer electron / shell			
	therefore outer electron lost more easily			
	*it must be stated that we are talking about outer electrons here at some point during the response. However, there is no need for it to be repeated			
	if not then any marking point regarding electron should **not** be given			
03.1	7		1	AO1 5.4.2.2
03.2	5		1	AO1 5.1.1.1

Question	Answer(s)	Extra info	Mark(s)	AO/Spec ref.
03.3	23 + 14 + (3 × 16) = 85	one mark for (3 × 16); two marks for correct answer, with or without working	1 / 1	AO2 5.3.1.2
03.4	nitric acid		1	AO2 5.4.2.2
03.5	nitric acid + sodium hydroxide → sodium nitrate + water	one mark for correct reactants (either order); one mark for correct products (either order)	2	AO2 5.4.2.2 5.1.1.1
03.6	$H^+ + OH^- \rightarrow H_2O$		1	AO1 5.4.2.4
04.1	protons = 1 / electrons = 1 / neutrons = 0		1 / 1 / 1	AO1 5.1.1.5
04.2	neutron relative mass = 1 / neutron charge = 0 / electron relative mass = 0 (or 1/2000, 1/1850 or other number of relative closeness to 0)	two marks for all correct; one mark for any two correct	2	AO1 5.1.1.4 5.1.1.5
04.3	**Level 3** a detailed explanation of why the relative atomic mass is 35.5, including calculation and description of atomic structure. A qualitative discussion of why the relative atomic mass is 35.5 and a detailed account of the atomic structure. Spelling and grammar used with accuracy nearly all of the time		5-6	AO3 5.1.1.5 5.1.1.6
	Level 2 a simple description of either atom and a qualitative treatment of the relative atomic mass. A quantitative calculation of the relative atomic mass of the sample. A detailed account of the structure of the atom. Spelling and grammar used with accuracy most of the time		3-4	
	Level 1 basic comment about isotopes. Good definition of isotope. Simple description of the structure of either Cl-35 / Cl-37. Basic qualitative RAM comment. Weak spelling and grammar		1-2	
	No relevant content		0	

Question	Answer(s)	Extra info	Mark(s)	AO/Spec ref.
	Indicative content **basic isotope information** same number of protons (ignore electrons) different number of neutrons **quantities of sub-atomic particles** Cl-35: 17 protons, 17 electrons and 18 neutrons Cl-37: 17 protons, 17 electrons and 20 neutrons Cl-37: two more neutrons **relative atomic mass of chlorine** more Cl-35 than Cl-37 (therefore) relative atomic mass closer to Cl-35 35 × 75 (= 2625) 37 × 25 (= 925) (2625 + 925) ÷ 100 = 35.5			
05.1		one mark for one shared pair; one mark for correct outer shell	2	AO2 5.2.1.4
05.2	weak intermolecular forces / low boiling point / little energy needed to overcome these forces		1 / 1	AO2 5.2.2.4
05.3	sodium atom loses 1 electron... / ...and becomes an ion with a charge of 1+ / fluorine atom gains 1 electron... / ...and becomes an ion with a charge of 1–	.	1 / 1 / 1 / 1	AO2 5.2.1.2
06.1	a reaction that transfers energy to the surroundings, and increases their temperature	accept a reaction that 'gives out' energy	1	AO1 5.5.1.1
06.2	diagram should show reactants higher than products	ignore any labels other than reactants and products	1	AO2 5.5.1.2
06.3	–5	one mark for – (minus); one mark for 5	1 / 1	AO2 5.5.1.2

Question	Answer(s)	Extra info	Mark(s)	AO/Spec ref.
06.4	two marks for all four temperature changes drawn accurately (only accept temp changes, not start / end temps); only one mark for 3 temperature changes drawn accurately one mark for suitable x-axis including labelling one mark for suitable y-axis including labelling		4	AO2 5.5.1.2 WS3.1
06.5	data is not just continuous / numeric, or words to that effect, e.g. x-axis data is not continous		1	AO2 5.5.1.2 WS2.2
06.6	Reaction = C Explanation = any one from: C only went up 10° so will get warm but not too hot. D goes up by 28° which could burn the skin. A does not increase enough. B is an endothermic reaction		1 1	AO3 5.5.1.1
07.1	carbon		1	AO1 5.2.3.3
07.2	**Level 3:** a linked explanation for both the electrical conductivity and high melting point and strength. Spelling and grammar used with accuracy nearly all of the time		5-6	AO2 5.2.3.1 5.2.3.2 5.2.3.3
	Level 2: basic comment made regarding conductivity and melting point and strength. Linked explanation for either electrical conductivity or melting point. Spelling and grammar used accurately most of the time		3-4	
	Level 1: basic comment about either conductivity or melting point and strength. Spelling and grammar used with high levels of inaccuracy		1-2	
	No relevant content		0	
	Indicative content **Electrical conductor** each carbon atom is bonded to three others has a free / delocalised electron... ...which can carry a charge (through the structure) **High melting point / strong** giant structure covalent bonds strong bonds require lots of energy to break them			

Question	Answer(s)	Extra info	Mark(s)	AO/Spec ref.
08.1	molten magnesium chloride a solution of potassium iodide	both answers required more than two ticks negates the mark	1	AO1 5.4.3.1 5.4.3.2 5.4.3.4
08.2	chlorine		1	AO2 5.4.3.4
08.3	hydrogen ions are positive and opposite charges attract	hydrogen ions are positive / opposite charges attract alone is not enough for the mark	1	AO2 5.4.3.1 5.4.3.4
08.4	sodium is more reactive than hydrogen (sodium reacts with water to make sodium hydroxide; hydrogen does not react with water)	accept converse	1	AO1 5.4.3.4
08.5	hydrogen gains one electron		1	AO2 5.2.1.2

Set B – Chemistry: Paper 4

Question	Answer(s)		Mark(s)	AO/Spec ref.
01.1	[3] — Anaerobic digestion of sewage sludge 1 — Screening and grit removal 4 — Aerobic biological treatment of effluent 2 — Sedimentation to produce sludge and effluent	2 marks for three correct answers; 1 mark for one or two correct	2	AO1 5.10.1.3
01.2	potable (water)		1	AO1 5.10.1.2
01.3	adding chlorine using ultraviolet light		1 1	AO1 5.10.1.2
01.4	distillation		1	AO1 5.10.1.2
01.5	X	more than one tick negates the mark	1	AO1 5.10.1.2
01.6	Y	more than one tick negates the mark	1	AO1 5.10.1.2

Question	Answer(s)		Mark(s)	AO/Spec ref.
02.1	oxygen	more than one tick negates the mark	1	**AO2** 5.9.1.1
02.2	79%	more than one tick negates the mark	1	**AO1** 5.9.1.1
02.3	any two from: burn/use fewer fossil fuels increase renewable energy use switch off electrical appliances ensure we have double glazing have your thermostat set low use low energy/ more efficient appliances/ light bulbs allow any other sensible suggestion to reduce carbon footprint	accept any suitable answer but both answers must be different	2	**AO1** 5.9.2.4
02.4	levels of oxygen (generally) increase		1	**AO3** 5.9.1.3
	slow increase until 600 million years ago (a 9 percentage point rise since 1000 million years ago)		1	
	between 400 million and 200 million years ago the levels fell again (but then increased again)		1	
02.5	algae/plants began to grow and carry out photosynthesis	ignore any comment about CO_2	1	**AO2** 5.9.1.3
	algae/plants release oxygen		1	
03.1	$2H_2O_2 \rightarrow 2H_2O + O_2$	1 mark for reactant 1 mark for products 1 mark for balancing	3	**AO2** 5.6.1.4 5.1.1.1
03.2	add a glowing splint		1	**AO1** 5.8.2.2
	relights if oxygen is present		1	

Question	Answer(s)		Mark(s)	AO/Spec ref.
03.3	hydrogen — squeaky pop is heard chlorine — damp litmus paper is bleached carbon dioxide — limewater turns cloudy	three correct for 2 marks; two correct for 1 mark; no marks for only one correct	2	**AO1** 5.8.2
04.1	2 – most of the crude oil evaporates and the vapours enter the column 5 – vapours that don't condense escape out the top of the column 1 – crude oil is heated to around 350 °C [3] – crude oil that didn't evaporate runs off at the bottom of the column 4 – the vapours condense at their own boiling point	four correct for 2 marks; two or three correct for 1 mark; no marks for only one correct	2	**AO2** 5.7.1.2
04.2	E		1	**AO3** 5.7.1.2
04.3	A		1	**AO3** 5.7.1.3
04.4	the longer the carbon chain, the higher the boiling point	accept converse	1	**AO1** 5.7.1.3
04.5	each fraction is a mixture	accept 'not pure'	1	**AO2** 5.8.1.1
04.6	LPG evaporates first when crude oil is heated	three ticks negates 1 mark	1	**AO2** 5.2.2.1
	fuel oil has the highest boiling point	four ticks negates both marks	1	
05.1	chromatography		1	**AO1** 5.8.1.3
05.2	any two from: line must be drawn in pencil line must be above solvent line must be drawn with a ruler		2	**AO2** 5.8.1.3
05.3	three		1	**AO2** 5.8.1.3
05.4	E110 and E111 (both required)		1	**AO2** 5.8.1.3
	dots are at the same level/ dyes have travelled the same distance		1	
05.5	insoluble (in water)		1	**AO2** 5.8.1.3

Question	Answer(s)		Mark(s)	AO/Spec ref.
05.6	distance moved by E112 = 31 mm	accept 29–33	1	AO2 5.8.1.3
	distance moved by solvent = 43 mm	accept 41–45	1	
	31 ÷ 43 (allow ecf from distances above)		1	
	0.72 (allow ecf from distances above)		1	
06.1	any one from: volume of acid concentration of acid length/size of magnesium	do not accept amount of magnesium	1	AO2 5.6.1.2
06.2	use a measuring instrument with a higher resolution OR weigh the magnesium		1	AO3 5.6.1.2
06.3	ignore anomaly (70 s)	allow 59 for 2 marks	1	AO2 5.6.1.1
	calculate mean (60 + 57 ÷ 2) = 58.5	allow 62 or 62.3 for one mark	1	
06.4	all points plotted correctly	one error for 1 mark	2	AO1 5.6.1.2
	line of best fit drawn correctly	no marks for more than one error	1	
07.1	carbon	or vice versa	1	AO2 5.7.1.1
	hydrogen		1	
07.2	combustion	ignore complete or incomplete accept exothermic do not accept burning	1	AO1 5.9.3.1 5.5.1.1
07.3	**Level 3:** a comprehensive answer which identifies the correct conditions, the correct drawings and the correct chemical test and result. Although one of the three parts may be incomplete they have accessed Level 3 by discussing each point to some level of correctness		5-6	AO2 5.7.1.4
	Level 2: an answer which contains some relevant points about two of the conditions, the chemical test or correct drawings. Some detail is missing and the explanation of the process may be incomplete		3-4	
	Level 1: an answer which contains some relevant points about conditions, the chemical test or correct drawings		1-2	

Question	Answer(s)		Mark(s)	AO/Spec ref.
	No relevant content		0	
	Indicative content **conditions** high temperature catalyst present (ignore named specific catalyst) **products**			
	(double bond can be anywhere but formula must be C_5H_{10}) **chemical test** add bromine water pentene/alkene will decolourise bromine water (accept colourless; do not accept clear)			
08.1	as concentration of acid increases, time taken for magnesium to react decreases	accept rate increases as concentration of acid increases	2	AO2 5.6.1.2
08.2	more particles in a given space / area	accept 'particles have more chance of collision'; ignore 'particles will collide more'	1	AO1 5.6.1.3
	frequency of successful collisions increases		1	
			1	
08.3	**Level 3:** a workable plan including concentration of acid and measurement of rate and fair testing and safety precautions.		5-6	AO2/3 5.6.1.2 5.6.1.3
	Level 2: a plan including concentration of acid of acid and should include an attempt at measuring rate and / or an attempt at fair testing and safety		3-4	

Question	Answer(s)	Mark(s)	AO/Spec ref.
	Level 1: a simple plan without reference to changing any variable but should include an attempt at measuring rate or an attempt at fair testing	1-2	
	No relevant content	0	
	Indicative content **plan** • add magnesium to acid • time reaction / 'count bubbles' / measure volume of gas • valid measurements given • change concentration of acid • suitable safety measures in place, e.g. wear safety goggles **control variables** • amount / mass / length / same 'size' of magnesium • volume / amount of acid		

Set B – Physics: Paper 5

Question	Answer(s)	Extra info	Mark(s)	AO/Spec ref.
01.1	alpha		1	AO1 6.4.2.1
01.2	alpha		1	AO1 6.4.2.1
01.3	beta		1	AO1 6.4.2.1
01.4	gamma		1	AO1 6.4.2.1
01.5	gamma		1	AO1 6.4.2.1
01.6	beta		1	AO1 6.4.2.1
02.1		1 mark for ammeter in a complete circuit 1 mark for voltmeter in parallel with X in a complete circuit. 1 mark for variable resistor in main circuit	3	AO1 6.2.1.4
02.2	charge = 0.12 × 10 charge = 1.2	1 mark for substitution 1 mark for answer	2	AO2 6.2.1.2
	unit: C	Correct answer with no working shown = 2 marks correct unit = 1 mark (independent)	1	AO1 6.2.1.2

Question	Answer(s)	Extra info	Mark(s)	AO/Spec ref.
02.3	any two from: as pd increases, current increases at higher pds, a (specific) increase in pd produces a smaller increase in current current approaches a limiting value component X is not an ohmic conductor resistance of component X increases as current increases at a pd of more than 0.7 V resistance of component X is constant up to a pd of 0.7 V	1 mark each for any two allow voltage instead of potential difference accept any other conclusion consistent with the pattern shown by the graph	2	AO3 6.2.1.3 6.2.1.4
03.1	**Level 2:** coherent and detailed comparison of the two models		3–4	AO1 6.4.1.3
	Level 1: some relevant information. Response may not be coherently structured, lack detail or include some incorrect points		1–2	
	No relevant content		0	
	Indicative content: both models include positive and negative charge plum pudding model: atom is a ball of positive charge nuclear model: Positive charge (accept mass) concentrated in small central nucleus plum pudding model: electrons embedded throughout (ball of) positive charge nuclear model: electrons surround the positive charge (nucleus) in a cloud (in orbit around)			
03.2	neutron proton	accept either order	1 1	AO1 6.4.1.3
04.1	(nuclei of the) same element with a different number of neutrons or (nuclei that have the) same number of protons but different number of neutrons		1	AO1 6.4.1.2
04.2	$^{222}_{86}Rn \rightarrow {}^{218}_{84}Po + {}^{4}_{2}He$	1 mark for substitution of each missing number	2	AO2 6.4.2.2
04.3	$^{218}_{84}Po \rightarrow {}^{218}_{85}At + {}^{0}_{-1}e$	1 mark for substitution of each missing number	3	AO2 6.4.2.2

Question	Answer(s)	Extra info	Mark(s)	AO/Spec ref.
05.1	they generate heat/they contain a heating element		1	AO3 6.2.4.2
05.2	printer		1	AO3 6.2.4.2
05.3	live — green and yellow stripes / blue — neutral / earth — brown (cross-matched lines)	1 mark for 1 correct 2 marks for 2 or more correct a maximum of 3 lines drawn	2	AO3 6.2.4.2
05.4	earth		1	AO1 6.2.3.2
05.5	live		1	AO1 6.2.3.2
05.6	power = (current)^2 × resistance		1	AO1 6.2.4.1
05.7	power = 4^2 × 2 power = 32 (W)	1 mark for substitution 1 mark for answer correct numerical answer with no working shown = 2 marks	2	AO2 6.2.4.1
06.1	a cup of tea cooling down — gravitational potential energy to kinetic energy / elastic potential energy to thermal energy / a falling football — thermal energy dissipated to the surroundings / a car braking — kinetic energy to thermal energy	1 mark for each correct line a maximum of 3 lines	3	AO1 6.1.1.1 6.1.2.1
06.2	elastic potential energy		1	AO1 6.1.1.2
06.3	(elastic potential energy = 0.5 × spring constant × (extension)^2) $E_e = \frac{1}{2} \times 25 \times 0.12^2$ energy stored = 0.18 (J)	1 mark for substitution into correct equation 1 mark for answer correct answer with no working shown = 2 marks	2	AO2 6.1.1.2
07.1	thermistor		1	AO1 6.2.1.1
07.2	as the temperature increases, the resistance decreases		1	AO3 6.2.1.4
07.3	the ammeter reading would increase		1	AO2 6.2.1.4
	because the total resistance in the circuit decreases (and $I = \frac{V}{R}$)		1	
07.4	400 (Ω)		1	AO2 6.2.1.4
07.5	total resistance (= $R_1 + R_2$) = 1200 Ω	allow ecf from 07.4	1	AO2 6.2.2
07.6	potential difference = current × resistance	accept V = IR	1	AO1 6.2.1.3
07.7	6.0 = current × 1200 current = $\frac{6.0}{1200}$ current = 0.005 (A)	1 mark for substitution 1 mark for rearranging 1 mark for answer correct answer with no working shown = 3 marks allow ecf from 07.5	3	AO2 6.2.1.3
08.1	thermometer C		1	AO3 6.1.1.3
	because it covers the required temperature range / B cannot cover range		1	
	and has the best (smallest) resolution (in that range) / can measure smaller temperature range than A or D		1	
08.2	temperature rise = 41.5 – 18.5 = 23.0 (°C) (accept 23)		1	AO3 6.1.1.3
08.3	(change in thermal energy = mass × specific heat capacity × temperature change) 21260 = 1.00 × c × 23.0 $c = \frac{21260}{1.00 \times 23.0}$ c = 924 (.348) J/kg°C answer given to 3 significant figures	1 mark for substitution in correct equation 1 mark for rearranging 1 mark for answer correct answer with no working shown = 3 marks 1 mark for correct answer given to 3 significant figures	3	AO2 6.1.1.3
			1	
08.4	aluminium		1	AO3 6.1.1.3
08.5	aluminium		1	AO3 6.1.1.3
08.6	brass		1	AO3 6.1.1.3

Question	Answer(s)	Extra info	Mark(s)	AO/Spec ref.
09.1	**Level 3:** a coherent plan covering all major steps presented in a logical order detailing all the apparatus used. The plan could be followed by another person to obtain a valid result for the density of the oil		5–6	AO2 6.3.1.1
	Level 2: a clear plan covering most of the major steps presented in a logical order detailing the apparatus used. The plan could be followed by another person to obtain valid results for the mass and volume of the oil		3–4	
	Level 1: some relevant statements but the plan could not be followed by another person to obtain valid results		1–2	
	No relevant content		0	
	Indicative content: mass of empty measuring cylinder measured mass measured with (electronic) balance oil poured into measuring cylinder volume of oil in measuring cylinder recorded mass of measuring cylinder with oil measured (with balance) mass of oil found by subtracting the mass of the empty measuring cylinder from the mass of the cylinder with oil density found by dividing the mass of oil by the volume avoid systematic errors by reading the measuring cylinder at eye level or taking account of the meniscus or ensuring the balance is zeroed			
09.2	take repeat measurements		1	AO3
	calculate an average value for the density		1	6.3.1.1

Set B – Physics: Paper 6

Question	Answer(s)	Extra info	Mark(s)	AO/Spec ref.
01.1	gamma		1	AO1 6.6.2.1
01.2	ultraviolet		1	AO1 6.6.2.4
01.3	gamma		1	AO1 6.6.2.3
01.4	Infrared Microwave (either order)		1 1	AO1 6.6.2.4
01.5	ultraviolet		1	AO1 6.6.2.3
01.6	microwaves		1	AO1 6.6.2.4

Question	Answer(s)	Extra info	Mark(s)	AO/Spec ref.
01.7	any two from: X-ray procedures are a risk to health / can cause (fatal) cancer X-ray procedures on different parts of the body present different sized risks the higher the X-ray dose, the longer the equivalent period of background radiation the risk of any single X-ray procedure is less than the risk of a 2-week period of background radiation	any two for 1 mark each accept any other sensible conclusion consistent with the data	2	AO3 6.6.2.3
02.1	velocity of an object is its speed in a given / specific direction	allow 'speed is a scalar, velocity is a vector'	1	AO1 6.5.4.1.3
02.2	1.5 m/s		1	AO1 6.5.4.1.2
02.3	three different stages in the following order: constant acceleration, constant velocity, constant deceleration/ negative acceleration **or** acceleration of 5 m/s²; constant velocity of 15 m/s; deceleration of 7.5 m/s²/ acceleration of -7.5 m/s² **or** correct time intervals specified for acceleration, constant velocity, deceleration in that order	1 mark for each statement maximum 3 marks	3	AO3 6.5.4.1.5
02.4	1 minute = 60 s distance travelled = 90 × 60 distance travelled = 5400 (m)	1 mark for unit conversion 1 mark for substitution 1 mark for answer Correct answer with no working shown = 3 marks	3	AO2 6.5.4.1.2
03.1	distance travelled by the car during the driver's reaction time.		1	AO1 6.5.4.3.1

Question	Answer(s)	Extra info	Mark(s)	AO/Spec ref.
03.2	any one from: tiredness / drugs / alcohol / (a named source of) distraction (such as a mobile phone)	Any one for 1 mark	1	AO1 6.5.4.3.2
03.3	distance travelled by the car while the brakes are being applied		1	AO1 6.5.4.3.1
03.4	any one from: wet road / icy road / condition of tyres / condition of brakes / gradient of road / surface of road	any one for 1 mark	1	AO1 6.5.4.3.3
03.5	kinetic energy to thermal energy	only one box ticked	1	AO1 6.5.4.3.4
03.6	either: temperature of brakes rises / or: brakes become worn	either statement for 1 mark	1	AO1 6.5.4.3.4
03.7	thinking distance: increases steadily with increasing speed / braking distance: increases with increasing speed / (braking distance) at an increasing rate		1 / 1 / 1	AO3 6.5.4.3.1
04.1	according to Newton's **Third** Law, the bench exerts a force on the book equal in size to the book's **weight** / the force of gravity is a type of **non-contact** force	1 mark for each correctly substituted term	3	AO1 6.5.4.2.3 6.5.1.2
04.2	weight = mass × gravitational field strength	accept W = mg	1	AO1 6.5.1.3
04.3	500 g = 0.500 kg / weight = 0.500 × 9.8 / weight = 4.9 (N)	1 mark for unit conversion / 1 mark for substitution / 1 mark for answer / correct answer with no working shown = 3 marks	3	AO2 6.5.1.3
04.4	work done = force × distance moved (along line of action of force)	Accept W = Fs or W = Fd	1	AO1 6.5.2

Question	Answer(s)	Extra info	Mark(s)	AO/Spec ref.
04.5	100 cm = 1.00 m / work done = 4.9 × 1.00 / work done = 4.9 / unit: N m or J	1 mark for unit conversion / 1 mark for substitution and answer / correct answer with no working shown = 2 marks / allow error carried forward from 04.3 / 1 mark for unit	2 / 1	AO2 6.5.2 / AO1 6.5.2
05.1	1.5 m	only one box ticked	1	AO1 6.6.1.2
05.2	transverse		1	AO1 6.6.1.1
05.3	wave speed = frequency × wavelength	Accept $v = f\lambda$	1	AO1 6.6.1.2
05.4	frequency = 30 ÷ 15 = 2.0 Hz / wave speed = 2.0 × 1.5 / wave speed = 3.0 (accept 3) / unit: m/s	1 mark for frequency correctly calculated / 1 mark for substitution / 1 mark for answer / correct answer with no working shown = 3 marks / allow error carried forward from 05.1 / 1 mark for unit	3 / 1	AO2 6.6.1.2 / AO1 6.6.1.2
06.1	independent variable: (resultant) force / dependent variable: acceleration / control variable: mass (of glider) (accept: same glider or same air track set up)		1 / 1 / 1	AO3 6.5.4.2.2
06.2	(standard) weights (attached to the string hanging over the pulley)		1	AO1 6.5.4.2.2
06.3	glider moves freely/more smoothly / because friction removed/reduced		1 / 1	AO1 6.5.4.2.2
06.4	acceleration = $\dfrac{0.20^2 - 0.10^2}{(2 \times 0.5)}$ / acceleration = 0.030 (m/s²) (accept 0.03)	1 mark for substitution / 1 mark for answer / correct answer with no working shown = 2 marks	2	AO2 6.5.4.1.5

Question	Answer(s)	Extra info	Mark(s)	AO/Spec ref.
06.5	the relationship between force and acceleration is linear doubling the force doubles the acceleration force and acceleration are directly proportional	1 mark for one of the statements	1	AO3 6.5.4.2.2
06.6	(resultant) force = mass × acceleration	accept F = ma	1	AO1 6.5.4.2.2
06.7	substitution of data from one data set into F = ma, e.g. 0.020 = m × 0.040 $m = \dfrac{0.020}{0.040}$ mass of glider = 0.50 (kg) (accept 0.5)	1 mark for substitution 1 mark for rearranging 1 mark for answer correct answer with no working shown = 3 marks	3	AO2 6.5.4.2.2
07.1	show that nail is attracted to the core/electromagnet when switch closed/current flowing. observe nail fall when switch opened		1 1	AO2 6.7.2.1
07.2	**Level 3:** a coherent plan presenting all steps in a logical sequence. The plan could be followed by another person to obtain valid results. A safety procedure included. a procedure to achieve accurate data must be included to achieve the maximum mark		5–6	AO2 6.7.2.1
	Level 2: a clear plan presented in a logical order. The plan could be followed by another person to obtain valid results		3–4	
	Level 1: some relevant statements but the plan could not be followed by another person to obtain valid results		1–2	
	No relevant content		0	

Question	Answer(s)	Extra info	Mark(s)	AO/Spec ref.
	Indicative content: close the switch adjust the variable resistor to set the current to a chosen value record ammeter reading choose an ammeter with an appropriate resolution for the range of current readings (use trial runs as necessary) gradually add masses in small increments to the bar until the bar falls care should be taken to avoid injury e.g. to feet when the iron bar and masses fall by placing soft material below the electromagnet add the weight of the bar to the weight of the masses attached to the bar to get the attractive force exerted by the electromagnet repeat the procedure and calculate an average total weight for that current repeat with several different current values to produce several data sets of current and total weight/ attractive force			
07.3	4.2 5.2	1 mark for both values correct	1	AO2 6.7.2.1
07.4	two points correctly plotted straight line of best fit drawn that passes through origin	1 mark for both points correct 1 mark for suitable line of best fit allow error carried forward from 07.3	2	AO2 6.7.2.1
07.5	increasing the current increases the strength of the electromagnet and either: the strength is directly proportional to the current or: doubling the current doubles the strength	1 mark for a basic conclusion or 2 marks for a conclusion referring to direct proportionality	2	AO3 6.7.2.1

BLANK PAGE

BLANK PAGE

BLANK PAGE